D0770574

Finding Myself,
Finding My Daughter

Cheryle (Shelly) Riedmann

Finding Myself, Finding My Daughter

✦

An Open And Honestly Written Journal About a Woman's Struggle To First Find Herself and then Her Adopted Daughter.

Cheryle Ann Rietmann

iUniverse, Inc.
New York Lincoln Shanghai

Finding Myself, Finding My Daughter
An Open And Honestly Written Journal About a Woman's Struggle To First Find Herself and then Her Adopted Daughter.

Copyright © 2005 by Cheryle Ann Rietmann

All rights reserved. No part of this book may be used or reproduced by any means, graphic, electronic, or mechanical, including photocopying, recording, taping or by any information storage retrieval system without the written permission of the publisher except in the case of brief quotations embodied in critical articles and reviews.

iUniverse books may be ordered through booksellers or by contacting:

iUniverse
2021 Pine Lake Road, Suite 100
Lincoln, NE 68512
www.iuniverse.com
1-800-Authors (1-800-288-4677)

ISBN-13: 978-0-595-36949-2 (pbk)
ISBN-13: 978-0-595-81358-2 (ebk)
ISBN-10: 0-595-36949-9 (pbk)
ISBN-10: 0-595-81358-5 (ebk)

Printed in the United States of America

To Gregg, thank-you for sharing the journey and for not trying to change me. I love you.

Contents

Introduction

When I began writing this journal, my purpose was to tell the story of the long journey to find my beautiful adopted daughter. I started trying to identify the first moment I felt the almost "desperate" longing to find this lost and lonely little girl that I somehow knew was out there waiting for me. I began to see the parallels in the search to find my daughter and the search to find myself. With love and perseverance we did find our way home and to each other.

It's hard to pinpoint the exact moment "Ola" popped into my heart. Of course, I didn't know it was "Ola" at first, but I always thought that someday I would adopt. I have always loved children and ached for the ones who didn't have a family. Every child deserves a family, even if that family is not perfect. Someone who loves you no matter what.

I am the oldest of four girls in my family. I was born prematurely, almost a month early, which is typical of me as I am always in a hurry to get to "the next big thing"! My father tells me I came out "staring at him in a suspicious manner", with my little finger out in perfect "lady like" form. He new immediately he was "in big trouble"! I was seldom called Cheryle growing up, unless I was in trouble! My family called me Shelly or "Shell-Bell" most of the time. One of the most wonderful memories I have of growing up was when my younger sisters were born. My sister Melissa was born when I was ten years old and I remember all the excitement! I'd wake up to her crying in the middle of the night and run up the stairs from my bedroom in the basement. I'd sweep her up in my arms and cuddle with her. I'd race to get there before my mom would, so that I could be the one to comfort her. The connection I felt with her was the most wonderful form of love I had ever known. I still think the love you receive from a child is comparable to no other.

My sister Sandi was born when I was twelve and it was just as fun and exciting with her. My sister Lori and I, who were closer in age (less than two years apart), like to tease my mom about how "WE" actually raised our two younger sisters. We had so much fun with them. We even took them on many of our dates! I've always felt very comfortable caring for babies. It came natural for me. I have a huge sense of rage when I think of neglected, abused, or abandoned children.

I had a very comfortable and some would say "pampered" childhood. My father was a farmer in rural eastern Oregon. We had a nice home and lots of room to run around. We never wanted for much. My dad raised wheat, and we also had cows. My best friend was my horse "Pepsi". We had a pond to fish in and ice skate on. I remember as a little girl complaining that the frogs were "too loud" and that they kept me awake at night! We went to the river every Sunday in the summer to boat and water ski.

I enjoyed going to stay at my grandparents' house not far away. They were also farmers and I was very close to them. I loved to sleep with them as my grandma used to kiss all my fingers and toes over and over again until I fell asleep! I had lots of cousins and have wonderful memories of growing up in a large family.

My father had a lot of pressure and responsibility thrown on him at a young age. His father died when he was only twenty years old. Right out of college my dad went straight to taking over the family ranch. At twenty-three he was married, had a baby on the way, and also had his mother living with them. Although my father worked a lot we loved evenings when he was home, in a good mood, and ready to play with us. Our favorite game was when he would be the "bucking bull"! With us on his back holding on tight he'd try to "buck us off" (not very hard, I suspect). My mother was a traditional stay-at-home mom. She was a great cook and always had cookies and other goodies waiting for us when we got off the school bus, a luxury I'm sure I didn't appreciate at the time.

Happy times in my childhood

Although I look back on my childhood with many fond memories and with a great deal of gratitude, it is shadowed by my fathers temper. My Dads volatile personality caused a great deal of tension in our home while I was growing up. Often no one knew there was a frightened child hiding in the corner or at the bottom of the stairs, listening to the yelling and crying. Not only were there household items being broken, but also little pieces of my heart. I, being the oldest, probably bore the brunt of my father's temper. I "paved the way" for my three younger sisters by pushing everything I did to the limit.

I was a very strong-willed, creative, and somewhat hyperactive child. Not a good combination to pair with a "short-fused" father. I'm not sure if my cousins looked forward to, or dreaded, the yearly Christmas pageants that I wrote, directed, and of course starred in. This was one of the many "huge" events I felt responsible for making sure happened.

The problem with passionate people is they usually aren't very content people. People like myself need to be busy, creative, and smack dab in the middle of something "big" at all times! We can be difficult to watch and deal with, let alone love. But I do believe it takes passionate people to make things happen. Hopefully, we are worth the extra patience needed to put up with us.

Patience is not a virtue my father has going for him. Combined with my headstrong personality and my father's temper our relationship got off to a very rough start. The clashes between us got uglier and uglier as I grew up. By the time I was fifteen, as it is with many teenagers, I thought I knew all I needed to know about life. In my parent's defense, I will admit I tested their patience to the max! I snuck out of the house, skipped school, stole many bottles of wine and disobeyed them almost on a daily basis! Even knowing how horrible my father's violent reaction could be, I continued with my wild behavior. With that said, I still believe I was not that different than many teenagers and it took years for me to know I did not deserve the physical and emotional violence I endured. I do realize how difficult it is for parents to know when kids need more discipline, more love, or a little of both! Parenting is not easy, but violence is never the answer.

My family was Catholic and many subjects were "black and white" issues, not open for discussion. Religion in my childhood wasn't a positive force for me, but more an added source of guilt and fear. My defiant personality combined with my father's temper, made for an explosive situation.

I started dating a boy older than I was when I was just fifteen and he was eighteen. Matt came from a large city and had much more of life's experiences under his belt. I was very infatuated by this. We became serious quickly. I think I just grabbed on and clung to this new feeling of love and affirmation. He was very popular in school and all the girls wanted to go out with him. I was very young, insecure, and inexperienced with boy's. I was flattered and surprised when he began paying attention to me. He was a drummer in a band and when you're a teenager that's very cool! Matt was very charismatic, but also a dominating and controlling person. He also had a very bad temper. The year I turned seventeen my life became a whirlwind of disaster and mistakes. My father and I seemed to be in constant conflict. Dating an older boy caused me to grow apart from my friends and participate less and less in school activities. The things I had enjoyed and that had made school fun, such as cheerleading, dance team, and theater, now seemed silly and childish. Because of all these things, my relationship with my parents deteriorated rapidly and I became more and more attached and dependent on my boyfriend.

I was very busy trying to grow up as fast as I could. I thought I was ready to take on the world. What should have been a fun, carefree time in my life, when I should have been working on my grades, attending prom, and graduating, ended up being the most stressful and devastatingly painful time of my life. I felt confused and pulled in every direction. I had so many big plans for my future but I was not strong enough, secure enough, let alone mature enough, to know how to achieve them.

My father jokes now about how bad it is when a father and his daughter are trying to "grow up" at the same time. My mother and I could not seem to talk without fighting either. My mother did not have the strength to stand up to my father's temper and often retreated to her own private and safe corner. She most likely didn't know how very much I needed her to reach out and hold on to me, even though I was pushing her away.

My mother, I think, was going through her own private hell, trying to be the "referee" between my father and me, but not wanting to get hurt herself. It was a very difficult time for all of us. I know I certainly did not understand everything that was happening at such a fast speed. I needed help sorting through the wide range of emotions I was feeling, and didn't know where to turn. I will always wish that I could have had someone neutral, calm, and wise to talk to during those years.

Teenagers need guidance. It is such an important time in life, a time when you have to make some of life's most difficult and important decisions. As a teenager you are just starting to feel all those very adult emotions and yet you are totally incapable of processing those emotions. I understand that these years are often the most difficult for parents. I may sometimes have been very difficult, but my father's violent reactions did not help the situation. It catapulted me into a life I was nowhere near ready for. I'd give anything for a "do over," but unfortunately that's not how life works. I realize now how much the choices you make when you're young can affect the rest of your life. I also know how anger and violence can scar a child for life and the effect on their self-esteem is often irreversible.

One afternoon after a terrible fight with my Dad, I left home. Although I acted tough and "in control," I was terrified and confused. The only thing I knew for sure was that I would never return home to live.

1

"Turbulent times"

Because a seventeen-year-old girl with no money usually has few places to go when she runs away from home, I ended up at my boyfriend's apartment. For the time being I felt safe there. I did love him and felt like he was the only one I could turn to. He was quite self-centered though. We talked mostly about "his" plans for the future. We never talked about my dreams.

I had applied to an arts program in Florida and had dreams of doing something in that field. I wanted to be an actress, a writer, a director, or maybe a fashion designer! Something "glamorous, creative, and exciting!" Matt made it very clear that if I thought I needed to go to some arts school in Florida, it would definitely be over between us. He wasn't open to my going to "any kind of school" for that matter! At that time, I thought he was the only thing I had in the whole world, and I didn't want to lose him. I swallowed all my ambitions and just hoped and believed that love would be enough. I wish so much that I had known I did have other options.

Matt thought things were great! I went straight to cleaning his apartment, doing the laundry, and cooking his meals. When I tried to explore career options for myself, or going back to school, he made me feel like I was being selfish. I did manage to complete high school and take a few college courses, but then realizing our financial situation, I knew I just needed to get a job. My heart ached for the real person trapped inside me. The person no one, including myself, knew how to reach.

I know now how important it is for each and every one of us to fulfill our OWN dreams. We cannot be truly happy if we're working only at fulfilling someone else's dreams. I also realize that the best time to explore who you are and where your place is in the world is when you're young, with no responsibilities and "optimally" with the strength and support of your family behind you. I gave that all up, and I'll always mourn that loss.

Around that time my grandfather that I so adored, died of cancer. He was the one I had always turned to as a child. He always had the love and patience I was looking for. He and my grandma were the ones who helped me with school projects and provided the extra love and attention I was looking for. Their home was a virtual safe haven for me.

His death brought me back home. I remember going to see my grandma the day my grandfather died. I crept into their dark bedroom to find her weeping in her bed. The bedroom that had always been so cozy, safe, and warm was now so dark and cold. I did not know what to say or do. She flung her arms around me and we cried. I will never forget the first words my grandmother said to me that day. "Your living with your boyfriend is breaking my heart," she cried. "You are hurting me even more than your grandfather dying! You have to at least get married if you're going to live with him."

She was obviously so upset by this. I felt like I'd been slugged in the stomach. The guilt was all but consuming. I was married a few months later. It seemed like a good solution at the time, I remember waking up two days after I was married. I was just seventeen, married, living in a singlewide trailer in a tiny town—no friends, no job, no nothing. What had I done with my life? I soon realized that there were few, if any, opportunities for me there. I felt so scared and alone. I cried all day. I was just starting to realize the reality of the choices I had made.

My marriage was "turbulent" to say the least. Matt went through many different jobs. We had absolutely no security. I can't even begin to count how many times we had to move. The places we called "home" were hardly the "castles" I had dreamed of as a little girl! I tried so hard to fix them up and make them livable.

One of our first homes was in the mountains and didn't even have running water. It did, however, have pack rats. I grew so tired of the pack rats chewing through the cupboards and eating all of our food that I slept on the couch sometimes at night with a pistol and shot at them! Luckily for the pack rats I was a terrible shot and did more damage to the trailer than to them! No one can accuse me of not trying to make the best of things during those times!

It was always quite clear that Matt's illusive music career was the most important thing to him. I was expected to support him emotionally and financially, no matter what! At one point he talked me into selling the brand new car my parents had helped us buy so that he could buy music equipment. The money for the car was used to purchase a new drum set, speakers, and microphones. The replacement car for me was on old, beat-up Ford with a hole in the floorboard.

Again, I knew not to complain. I did my best to find jobs here and there and usually did fairly well with the opportunities I was given. I worked in dental offices during the day and cleaned homes evenings and weekends. Unfortunately, a musician's lifestyle does not make for much of a family life. Late nights, drugs, and alcohol seem to become part of "that scene" all too often. I never knew who would walk through the door at night—the sweet, charming boy I loved, or the mean, withdrawn one who scared me to death. I just knew not to make him mad! Matt became increasingly violent. Our "on again, off again" relationship was anything but a marriage! The "ups" we had certainly did not outweigh the "downs." I know I made my share of mistakes, which added to the chaos. We were both so immature. I tried to be supportive, but I knew our lives were going nowhere fast. Nowhere that I wanted to go anyway!

As I grew up and became stronger and more independent, we fought more. Again, violence became a part of my life. I was often called horrible names, pushed around, hit and at one of our lowest times, I was choked to the point that I feared for my life. The terror seemed to always be followed by ME apologizing for making him angry or letting him down. Each time I would think it would get better if I tried harder, but it only got worse. He definitely had a hold on me that I could not break free from. I did not realize until much later in life, that "love does not need to be this hard or hurt this bad"! We finally divorced when I was in my early twenties. It was a painful, long breakup that left me a mess.

I didn't realize until later that the cycle of physical and emotional violence first with my father and then with my ex-husband had chipped away at my self-esteem and left me hollow inside. I believed everything was my fault, and that I totally deserved all the anger I somehow managed to always create in my life. The downward spiral in my head had begun.

2

"The black hole"

In the years following my divorce I tried hard to make something out of my life and get back on my feet. I felt so lost and alone! I remember reading a book about that time that said, "When you're really down and out, sometimes the best thing to do is change your focus and try to help someone else who's much worse off than you." In an effort to try and change my perspective, I decided to quit dwelling on my problems and do something to help others. I decided to go into the medical field. I was looking for something that would be rewarding and help fill some of the "emptiness" I felt.

I decided that working as an office nurse would be a positive place for me to put my love and energy. I had been working in the dental field but was no longer enjoying it. I was just so tired of looking at teeth all day! I decided to go back to school to become a Certified Medical Assistant, with additional certifications in lab and x-ray. It may not have been much in the way of college, but it was the best I could do at the time.

I worked during the day, went to school at night, and studied on the weekends. Passing the State of Oregon boards was my first real sense of accomplishment. I worked hard and tried to keep busy, but I still felt very alone most of the time. My self-esteem was so low. I was horrible at dating! I remember a friend asking me once, "Have you managed to date every jerk west of the Mississippi yet?" I think I came close! My sisters also shook their heads and said, "If Shelly walked into a room full of wonderful, nice, eligible bachelors, she would find the one and only jerk in the crowd and head straight for him!"

I always chose to date men that were very critical and controlling. I used to joke about how any man who had ever claimed to love me would immediately follow with "just a few things I needed to change about myself if they were going to be able to continue loving me." Then out would roll the twenty-page list of my "major flaws." It's very hard to find someone who can love you exactly as you are!

I had come to truly believe no one could ever really love me. I thought I was a stupid loser. I tried to hide the "real" me sometimes and be whoever the man I was dating wanted me to be, but that was way too much work! Besides, you can't hide from yourself for long. At the end of each relationship I was always hurt and blamed myself. The saying "You can't begin to love someone else until you've learned to love yourself first" is so true. I believed there was something so horrible about me that it just brought out the "violent nature" in men. I was truly unlovable.

Although my work as a medical assistant helped fill the void in my life a great deal, I still seemed to be on a constant emotional roller coaster. I moved around a lot, changed jobs, tried to find a place to call home, but never seemed to land anywhere that I felt I belonged. I worked hard to become what I thought was the perfect woman, but I always fell horribly short in my mind. I eventually became anorexic and bulimic. I hated what I saw in the mirror. I didn't know how to fix the "inside" of myself so I worked on the "outside." I exercised to excess. I drank way too much alcohol in an effort to "drown" the self-loathing, which of course only made things worse. Nothing I did seemed to ease the pain. I guess I had to totally hit "rock bottom" before I could finally start to climb out of the hole I had dug myself into.

"Rock bottom" for me was waking up in the ER, strapped to a cold, hard table, and looking up at a heart monitor—with charcoal and vomit all over my face and matted in my hair. I'm not sure you can really understand how people get to the point that they think suicide is the answer unless you've been there. I've heard people say "It's a cry for help" or that people "do it for attention" and "it's such a selfish act." Although all of these things may hold some truth, it is usually much more complicated than that.

Mental health is a lot more "fragile" than people want to believe. We live in such a competitive world. We are all expected from a very young age to be "strong, successful, and independent." Add to the mix the ridiculous images we project onto women, regarding their looks and sexuality. It's no wonder so many women become confused and depressed. How can we possibly live up to these unrealistic expectations?

I felt so alone for so long. I don't blame anyone but myself. My family tried to be there as best they could. Good friends came and went. I always felt like everyone around me was able to make a life for themselves; but not me. I kept wondering what I was doing wrong. I looking back with that "if I knew then, what I know now" perspective, of course I would do a lot of things differently. I don't mean to sound like I had it worse off than anyone else. I realize that a series of poor choices on my part was the main reason I ended up where I did. It was a slow "descending" into the very dark place where I ended up.

Many people do not realize the grip that depression and low self-esteem can have on someone. Sometimes no matter how hard you try, you get so low you just can't pull yourself back up on your own. It's like being on a very slippery slope. You keep trying to crawl up it but you lose your footing and slide back down again. I'd put on the façade of being fine, but I was anything but. Suicidal thoughts crept into my head more and more until I was convinced it was the only answer. After a fight with a man I had been dating had once again ended with violence and cruel words, I completely broke down. The cruel words he said, I had heard one too many times, and now I believed them. I was all of those horrible things and more and I deserved to be alone. No matter how hard I tried, I always seemed to end up alone and feeling awful about myself.

I felt like I just couldn't try anymore. I just wanted to go to sleep and never wake up. I remember feeling relieved and almost elated that night. I had finally come up with a solution! I had come up with a way to make the pain go away. I would just lie down and go to sleep forever. I didn't care where I went, just anywhere but here. I truly believed everyone would sigh with relief when I was gone.

I lay down in front of my fireplace that night, and as I drank my wine I began taking sleeping pills. Slowly, I felt calmer and calmer and the tears finally stopped. My plan was working perfectly. I was making the world go away, the pain was subsiding, and I was drifting off to "somewhere else." Suddenly my grandpa's face "popped" into my head! He did not look happy. I never wanted my grandpa to be disappointed in me. Startled and more awake now, I started to question my plan. I then felt compelled to call my mom. I started to feel guilty about how this might affect her! I needed to call and at least tell her I loved her. I felt I owed her at least that much. I would not tell her anything else, just that I loved her.

I could hardly dial the phone. My mom, of course, could tell in my voice that something was terribly wrong. Though I kept telling her I was fine, she got enough out of me to figure out what I was attempting. I hung up the phone, lay back down, and continued with the wine and sleeping pills. My mom was over two hundred miles away, so she and my sister Lori called 911, who contacted the emergency resources in my area.

The next thing I remember was the EMTs kicking down the door, and the rest is a blur. I was taken to, and treated at, a nearby hospital. This is when I woke up on the cold, hard table. Not one of my better moments. But this was a turning point for sure.

I now realize what a precious gift life is. I value my life and the treasures it has brought me. I'm not proud of that night and am actually very ashamed that I let myself get that low. I remember the desperation I felt though. When you overdose on alcohol and sleeping pills, it causes you to hallucinate. I lay there in a dark room, my body strapped to a table, unable to move at all, going in and out of the world.

The life I had been living spun around in my head. All I could see when I closed my eyes were angry faces. I lay there all night alone, with tears streaming down my face. I called for my dad; I kept hearing his voice and seeing his face and I'd yell at the nurses to let him in. It's still so interesting to me that I kept calling for my dad. Of all the people in my life, why would I call for my dad? Why is the relationship between daddies and their little girls so important? I wanted him to come to me; I wanted him to love me. I guess there are some scars that never heal!

Even though my dad never came, (and never even spoke with me about that night), I would come to realize, that it was not because he doesn't love me. I've had to learn and accept that people "are just who they are." I have come to see that I needed to separate the "father I love" from the "ugly temper I hate." To realize sometimes people don't know how to reach out to you, but that doesn't mean they don't care!

We all have our strengths and weaknesses. We are all struggling to do the best we can in life. It's an ongoing battle trying to become better people every day of our lives. Maybe we all need to try a little harder to help each other along the way.

After a fitful, painful night in the hospital, the morning finally came. I just wanted someone to come and take the tape off and let me up off the table. The nurse finally did come and un-tape me after I promised not to try to hurt myself again, which was so humiliating. She then helped me wash my face and comb my hair. I appreciated her tenderness and caring so much at that point. I just wanted to crawl like a baby into her arms and have her hold me. "You have to decide whether you want to live or die," she said. "It's that simple, and it's really all up to you."

I knew she was right. I had nowhere to run now, nowhere to hide! I had to face it all, and deal with it! I knew the road ahead would be difficult. I was ready now. I had to look deep inside and face the pain and anger once and for all. I had to quit "wallowing in my pain" and learn to be happy on my own. I knew I would need some help, but ultimately it was up to me.

3

"Coming out of the dark"

It didn't happen over night, but with some counseling and a lot of soul-searching I began to feel better about myself. I also realized that I had to forgive myself, my parents, my ex, and anyone who had ever hurt me or let me down. I had to quit looking back and blaming, and look forward with a positive heart and mind. Forgiveness is such an important part of life. People are always going to say and do things that hurt us, but hanging onto those bad feelings doesn't leave room in our heart for the good feelings. It's a lot of work being angry and resentful and a total waster of time and energy.

Time, I began to realize, is precious. It's not always easy to let go and move forward. I am still often plagued with self-doubt and anger as much as anyone, but I will never let it control my life again. Hurt and anger are inevitable parts of life, and there are times when you have to let your self feel those emotions, work through them the best you can, and then let them go. I do know how much reacting to them with violence only makes things worse. Violence, whether physical or emotional, can be devastating and permanent. How simple the words "forgive" and "forget" are, but often so difficult to achieve.

I began hiking and taking long walks. I became healthier physically and emotionally. I was still very lonely, but I started to heal and find some inner peace. I remember that when I turned thirty, it magnified all the losses and things missing in my life. I sometimes thought that maybe I would never have the life and family I had always dreamed of. I did not let myself go backwards though; I worked very hard on trusting God and prayed he would guide me. This was when I began to discover the power of my own spirituality.

I slowly became a stronger, happier, and more self-reliant person. I learned I could survive on my own, and even be happy. I quit trying to find myself in someone else's eyes and finally realized that although it sounds cliché, everything I was searching to find was right there inside me all the time.

The next few years I continued to work towards setting goals and rediscovering my own hopes and dreams. I gave a lot of thought about where I would like to settle. I really did want to be self-sufficient and build a life for myself on my own. I quit waiting for the knight in shining armor to come along. I often thought about trying to adopt a child. I read a lot about adopting. I wasn't sure I could do it by myself though. Although I knew I could give a child the love they needed I worried I might not be able to give them the financial security they deserved.

I could barely make ends meet for myself. Working as an office nurse was rewarding emotionally but not particularly rewarding financially. I realized that my dreams of being a mom would have to wait. If God had that planned for me, it would happen when he thought it was the right time and place.

I began enjoying and appreciating the family I did have. I leaned on my sisters and became close to my parents again. I loved coming home to the ranch and cooking for everyone. Deep down I still hoped that I would find someone special to share life with. I tried not to dwell on it though. I tried to enjoy every day, every moment, for the gift that it is. Slowly, I began to heal, love, and appreciate life. It was around this time that I met Gregg.

It was always fun to come home for the yearly St. Patrick's Day celebration that goes on in the small town I grew up in, Heppner, Oregon. I enjoyed getting to see family and friends. Late at night, the week-end of our St. Patrick's celebration, a mutual friend introduced me to Gregg. My first thought was that he was a very cute boy! He was younger than me and I remember thinking he might be fun to date, but certainly not anyone I would be serious about. In the beginning I was very unsure about whether I wanted to go out with Gregg. I actually have my father to thank for "forcing" me to go on our first date. Gregg called me while I was home visiting my parents one weekend. I was cooking up a big "Mexican feed" for my family and Gregg called to invite me to his house for a Barbeque. Upon overhearing me decline Gregg's invitation my father "lit into me"!! "The nicest guy in Morrow County asks you out and you decline"????? "You're not getting any younger" he says to me in a not so gentle tone!!! "OK", I told him, "but I don't even know where he lives." With much more enthusiasm than I have at this point, my father offers to drive me to Gregg's house himself!!! We showed up at Gregg's later (after getting lost) and my Dad jumps out of the car with a six pack of beer in hand, and say's "I hope you don't mind that I brought Shelly?!" My Dad and Gregg had a wonderful first date. I wasn't really included in much of the conversation, (which was mostly about farming) but was asked if I could "make the salad"?! With me very skeptical, this is how Gregg's and my relationship began. Our relationship got off to a rocky start. He was always late for our dates. He often called very late from the bars. I thought, "Oh, here we go again," another typical, self-centered male, wanting to use me and break my heart. My mind was saying, "Beware, beware."

We had so much fun when we got together though, that I decided to proceed cautiously. I think we were both surprised by how much we really did have in common. We loved music and going to concerts. We loved spending time with family and friends. As I got to know Gregg I began to see the classy, caring person he really was. We had the same roots in common with growing up in large families on farms in eastern Oregon. We came from the same backgrounds and so we had much the same perspective about life. Gregg had lost his mother to cancer just a few years before we met. I was touched by the way he talked about her, sometimes with tears in his eyes.

As in all relationships, you get to a turning point where you start to let someone see the deeper, more "real" side of yourself. This is the scary part! I think that for Gregg, losing his mom made him realize how short life is and what really matters. Like me, Gregg was looking for something to hold on to. I was so afraid to fall in love with Gregg. I was sure I'd just end up getting hurt again. I never thought someone as wonderful as Gregg could love someone like me. I think Gregg was just as scared. It was not easy for him to step up and make a commitment to us, but eventually he was able to.

We were married on August 10, 1991. I was so happy! My relationship with Gregg is deeper and stronger than anything I have ever known. Gregg is so committed, patient, and caring. I never knew this kind of unconditional love existed. Someone who loves you exactly how you are! Gregg tells me I saved his life and I believe he did the same for me. This is the kind of love that can "heal" a broken heart. This is the kind of love that gives you the strength to become the person you were meant to be. The foundation we built together has allowed us both to become better people.

We had two beautiful boys together. First Tanner, and then seventeen months later, Evan. Gregg took over his father's farm, and has worked hard towards expanding it into a solid and secure business. I've worked part-time, but mostly been a stay-at-home mom, our lives being centered around our kids.

As with all families, we have our ups and downs, but our faith and commitment to each other is always strong. Gregg never quits believing in me and it amazes me! For the most part we couldn't be happier. This is the kind of foundation needed when you set out to open your hearts and home to an adopted child. Something in my heart had never quit nagging at me! The thoughts of adopting had never gone away. The little voice in my head never quieted. It seemed to me that God had helped me to heal and grow and now he was asking me to help him with another child who needed to heal and grow. I believe he wanted me to share the beautiful life he had given me with a little one who needed and deserved it.

As I said before, I had always thought about adopting, but Gregg never had. Even when Gregg and I were first dating, I talked about how awesome I thought adoption was. Gregg never said too much but always seemed open to the idea. Our two boys are absolutely wonderful, sweet, kind, and generous children. We could not be prouder of them. Gregg and I both agree our children are the best things that ever happened to us. Tanner always has a million questions about everything in life. He is constantly "negotiating." Evan is more easy going and content, but also more emotional with a goofy sense of humor.

When Tanner was ten and Evan nine, the nagging feelings about adopting not only resurfaced but came back stronger than ever. I truly believed there was a child waiting somewhere for us. I've said many times to people that I was "supposed" to adopt; I always felt it, always knew it. I think maybe God chooses people and sprinkles "crazy dust" on them. It gets in your head and your heart and won't go away. The voice in my head that had always been there whispering to me about adopting, had now begun yelling. It had become almost impossible to ignore.

I didn't know it at the time, but at the same time the pull towards adopting was intensifying for me, our Ola was born! One night lying in bed I said to Gregg, "I want you to seriously think about adopting. We have two boys, so how about a little girl?" I told him that his decision needed to be 100 percent; there was no room for doubt. I told him I would not be angry if he didn't think he could do this, but that we needed to make a decision together once and for all.

He agreed to give it a lot of thought and let me know. We had talked about adoption often, but now it was time to decide. Only a few days went by and once again as we were lying in bed about to fall asleep, he announced that he "absolutely had no doubts whatsoever about adopting." He agreed that it felt "totally right and meant to be." Apparently, God had snuck in and sprinkled the "crazy dust" on him too!

4

"Preparing to adopt"

Gregg is such an awesome dad. I couldn't wait to see him with a daughter. I knew having a little girl would "soften" him in a way he had never known. He had been raised in a family of three boys; so I knew this would be a whole new world for him. I also thought it would be so good for the boys and hopefully make them a little less self-centered. Our world would broaden and our perspectives would expand with this experience.

After making the decision together to move forward we were both very excited. The next step was talking to the boys. We felt this needed to be a family decision and everyone had to be on board. If everyone didn't feel the same it wouldn't work. When we approached the boys we gave it to them straight. We never glamorized adoption. We told them there would be times when it would be hard. We explained that our adopted daughter, their sister, would hold exactly the same kind of place in our hearts as they did. We would love her the very same way that we loved them. We explained that we would not be able to "take her back" if they decided she was a pain! We did our best to explain all the possible problems an adopted child might have and how much extra love and attention she might need.

Our boys needed very little time to think about it. They were excited about adopting from the beginning. We had many long and open talks together as a family, and we all kept agreeing that we were ready to "go for it!" We had so much love in our family and felt blessed in so many ways, sharing it with a child who had no one and nothing would be wonderful.

Soon we began the long process of adopting. The boys immediately went to school and told everyone about their "coming new sister." Their teachers remarked how wonderful their attitudes and excitement were. It was funny when I began telling my sisters and close friends about our decision to adopt. More than once I began by saying, "I have something important to tell you," and my sisters and best friends jumped in with, "You're finally going to adopt, aren't you?" I was so surprised that they guessed it before I could tell them. I guess I had talked about adopting over the years more than I realized. Not everyone reacted positively, but most everyone close to us was supportive.

We had many fun conversations about how it would be with our new little girl. My aunt and uncle had adopted a little girl back when I was in my early twenties. Adrienne was such a beautiful baby girl and grew into a beautiful young lady. I remember when I got the phone call on Christmas Eve morning. I hadn't known my aunt and uncle were planning to adopt so I was surprised, but immediately excited. My mom called to tell me of her arrival and that her name was Adrienne. "She is so beautiful," my mom gushed. I couldn't wait to get home and see her.

I ran to the Emporium during my lunch hour and purchased the most adorable red velvet Christmas dress, white tights, and black patent leather shoes. The outfit I bought her was huge on her, but looked so cute. The red velvet up against her olive skin, dark hair, and dark eyes made her look even more gorgeous. This was our family's first experience with adoption.

From day one we could not have loved Adrienne more. She is a very special part of our family. One evening we were talking to the boys about the possibility that we might adopt a child from another country. We brought up the fact that she might be old enough to talk and that she might speak a different language than us. It could be hard for us to communicate at first. Evan jumped in with, "Oh, I know, mom, we can have Adrienne talk to her cuz she's adopted too!" After thinking a moment, he immediately got embarrassed and said, "Oh, that was stupid." It was so cute though. We still tease Evan a lot about that "universal adoption language." We shared it with Adrienne and she said she'd be more than happy to "translate" for us!

Our family was ready to begin our journey to find our little girl. We had no idea where she was and how to get to her. We also had no idea the lessons in love we would learn along the way. We really weren't even sure where to begin. We first began thinking we could find our little girl here in the United States. We started by taking the required classes on adoption and foster parenting. We signed up right away for classes nearby. They were on Saturdays and lasted all day.

The classes were very hard to sit through. They were government-run classes and were set up to prepare prospective foster and adoptive parents for any and all the problems adopted children can have. We would come to realize that most of the children that become available for adoption in the United States have been through some form of abuse. Unfortunately many of them have been victims of neglect, or physical or sexual abuse. Many of them have serious medical problems, such as fetal alcohol syndrome, or permanent damage from their mother's drug abuse during pregnancy.

It is heart breaking. We learned that the feelings of abandonment for these children can leave very deep scars. Often these children act out in very destructive ways. This is their way of coping and dealing with their pain. State programs do all they can to make sure that foster and adoptive parents are aware of these possible problems and are prepared to deal with them as best they can.

Adjusting to a new family can be very difficult for these children. Their negative behavior can be very hard for families to handle. The children almost always have huge "trust issues." It was hard to read about, watch videos about, and be lectured on child abuse for hours on end. It was depressing to say the least. Gregg and I worried about what we might be subjecting our boys to. When you begin the adoption process you need to do a lot of soul-searching and be very honest with yourselves. Everyone has their own limits in regards to what you and your family are able to handle as far as the "special needs" of these children.

We knew that we needed to be very honest and open, together as a family. We began looking every day at the Web pages of children available for adoption in our state and the other states that Oregon works with. Many months went by and we started to become disillusioned with the hope of finding a little girl through the State's system. It was sad and hard for us to accept the fact that most of the children who come up for adoption here in the United States have bigger problems than we were prepared to handle.

Finding just one healthy little girl with limited problems is rare. Most of the time there are two or three siblings to be placed for adoption and there has almost always been some form of abuse in the children's past. I am not saying that the children who come up for adoption here in the United States are not beautiful, wonderful, special children. All children are beautiful, wonderful, and special and they deserve permanent, loving homes. We just didn't seem to find the little girl who we felt was "supposed" to be ours.

We were not sure what we should do. We also looked at "open adoption," which is a very popular way to adopt these days. This is when the birth mother is allowed to select the parents or family for her unborn baby. Most of the time the mother can keep some form of contact with the family as the child grows up. This makes the decision of placing your unborn baby up for adoption a little more humane, and less painful for the birth mother. This is a great option for a woman who finds herself pregnant and decides she is unable to raise the child herself. This is a beautiful unselfish plan for families. Often this plan, although very emotional for both sides, works out wonderfully for everyone involved. But it brings with it a long list of emotional issues that need to be dealt with, with open hearts and open minds.

Although each situation is different, often families who choose open adoption need to be prepared to handle ongoing contact with the birth mother and often times extended family, meaning grandparents, aunts, uncles, etc. This makes this form of adoption a little more "complicated" and emotional and with its own set of issues. I so admire families who can make this work. Everyone involved must be willing and able to put the best interest of the child first.

Gregg and I considered open adoption very seriously. Since there is a long list of couples waiting to be chosen for an "open adoption," we did not want to take a child away from couples who were unable to have biological children of their own. We understood the desire to bond with a new baby from the moment they are born. We felt very fortunate that we had had that experience with the boys. Something told us we were supposed to go down a different road to find our child. This was when we began to look at international adoption.

We learned of all the orphans all over the world that desperately needed homes. For some reason this was the route we felt most pulled towards. Where in the world was she though? The world's a pretty big place! We wondered where to start. We first needed to decide what country we wanted to adopt from and which agency we wanted to work with. This is another difficult decision process you must go through when you decide to adopt.

I began reading and researching each country's programs. I used the Internet and the Yellow Pages to find names of adoption agencies. I muddled through tons of information. It was overwhelming, but we moved forward with great faith and the strong belief that there was a little girl out there waiting for us somewhere. I narrowed our search to a couple different countries and a couple different agencies. We had no idea that choosing an agency would be so hard. I thought we'd just "sign up somewhere" and be put on a waiting list. For some reason I was attracted to some of the smaller agencies. I hoped I could find one not too far away. I didn't want to be a "number" or just another "file folder." I wanted to be able to pick up the phone and call our worker with our questions. I wanted to feel like I knew them and they knew us.

If you've never been through the international adoption process you might not understand how hard it is to select the agency that will be guiding you on such an important journey. You have to trust them completely. This is so personal and there is so much at stake. I finally picked two agencies in the Portland area that had programs in the countries we were interested in. Before I made a final decision I felt I needed to go to each agency and meet with the people we would be working with. I wanted to meet face to face and then I would know if I could trust them. Old fashioned, maybe even naïve, but that's what I needed to do.

Unfortunately, many adoption agencies are in it for the money. So many hopeful adoptive parents fall victim to "unethical" agencies that take well-meaning families and basically "sell" children to them for financial gain. They take their money and good intentions and take total advantage of them. They make all kinds of promises that are impossible to achieve. I knew we needed to be very careful.

When I pulled into Journeys of the Heart Adoption Agency in Hillsboro, Oregon, I thought it looked more like a home than an agency. It is in an older home that has been remodeled into a place of business. The warm smiles and cozy atmosphere made me feel immediately at home. Susan, one of the owner/operators, met with me in a bright, sunny room off the main office area. Susan is a warm, caring, and open person. She was so easy to talk with. She made the visit feel very "personal.'

Susan wanted to know about me, my husband, the boys, and the specific dynamics that made up our family. She seemed genuinely sincere in helping us reach our dream of adopting a little girl. She gave a lot of thought to which country would be best for us and what age child would "fit" best into our family. She was really excited for us. I came away believing this was meant to be our agency. I felt safe and comfortable with them. In the end we would know that it was the right way to go. Although the path we took was a "bumpy one," it was the path we had to take to get to our girl.

We signed up with Journeys of the Heart Adoption Agency and armed with a ton of information regarding each of the countries they worked with, I headed for home. I stopped at Powell Book Store to pick up some geographical books and maps. To my embarrassment I was not even sure where some of these countries were. Why didn't I pay more attention in school? It was so interesting learning about each country and its culture. We'd found our agency and now we needed to make a decision about which country we'd adopt from. Again, we thought, "Where in the world is our little girl?"

At first Gregg thought it might be better to choose a child who looked similar to us. In the end I think we could have cared less about that. We first looked at Russia and Romania. We talked about China, because of all the little girls that need homes there. This was the time when the SARS epidemic broke out. Adoptions were closed down in China and even travel there was very limited so that was not an option. We gave serious consideration to every country and every program.

We finally settled on Romania. The children were beautiful, the program was moving along fairly well at the time, and we liked the idea of not having to travel there unless we chose to. The Romanian program at that time was set up so that you received "referrals" from Romania through your agency. After looking at your child's portfolio and seeing them through photos and/or videos, and then accepting your referral, a social worker would travel there for you, take care of all the paper work, and bring your child home to you. This saves a lot of time and money.

Many of the other countries we looked at had programs which required traveling to that country, sometimes more than once, and usually a lengthy stay in that country. Gregg and I enjoy traveling, but with two boys in school and a wheat ranch to run, a long stay in a foreign country can be a real hardship, not to mention expensive. So Romania it was. We were then assigned to a caseworker. His name was Radu. Gregg and I got a kick out of talking with Radu. He had a great accent, and his sentences were sort of choppy. He definitely knew his way around the Romanian program.

Radu is very committed to getting orphaned children in Romania homes. He and his wife are from Romania, so he was especially emotional and committed to Romania and Romanian children. The first thing we needed to do was set up a home study. We were referred to a social worker out of Hermiston, a town close to us. This was great because we wouldn't have to pay travel expenses for her to visit our home, which could add up to a good amount. Her name was Anne.

We were scheduled for our home study the first of April 2003. I was so nervous. Our house, our yard, our "lives," need to be in perfect order. I think I scrubbed my house from top to bottom for two weeks straight. Gregg even had to have the barnyard and his shop clean (not always the case with Gregg)! I knew safety would be an issue, so we went through all our cleaning supplies, medicine cabinets, etc., to make sure anything harmful was out of reach. We bought fire extinguishers and checked each and every fire alarm in our house.

Everything we thought we needed to do we did twice. I was so worried about something that might make us look "bad." The day finally came, the house and yard were in perfect order and we were ready and very nervous. Anne couldn't have been nicer. She was so easy to talk to. She was sweet and kind and walked us through the interview process painlessly. We actually enjoyed it! She brought the boys down to ask them a few questions.

Anyone who has had nine and ten year old boys will understand our anxiety at this point. We have awesome boys and they are very polite, but children can be so honest. Who knew what might come out of those precious boys' little mouths?! The boys, our home, all of us passed with flying colors. It was obvious to us and Anne that the boys were very excited about getting a sister and that they were going to make really great big brothers. We felt very good about our home study. Anne had it typed up and off to our agency quickly. She gave us a very good reference.

The next step was getting through the INS (U.S. Immigration and Naturalization Service). We filled out all the required paperwork and sent it off. I ran to the mailbox everyday hoping to see an envelope with the INS's return address on it. It seemed like it took forever but in realty it took about six weeks, which is actually pretty good for the INS, according to others who have waited much longer for clearance.

During that same time we also had to be fingerprinted and have all kinds of criminal background checks. Fingerprinting for me turned out to be a nightmare. By the time all was said and done I would be fingerprinted four times. Apparently my years as a medical assistant, which requires washing your hands many times a day, makes for "poor fingerprints." It seemed I had washed my fingerprints away!

After having them done three times, once by the INS in Portland and twice by local government offices in our area, and subsequently having them rejected I finally had had it and I drove to the State Police Department in Salem, Oregon. They have an electronic finger-printing machine that tells you on the spot whether each fingerprint will be accepted by the INS or not. After reaching the end of my rope with this whole fingerprinting issue, I finally just showed up at their office. This entailed a 500 mile round trip for me! I told them I would not be leaving until we had acceptable fingerprints.

One finger was particularly difficult; it had a "crack" in it, they said. I remember thinking, "A crack in my finger is keeping me from my daughter?" They actually felt sorry for me after hearing my story and were very accommodating. We were finally successful. Accepted fingerprints; now on to the next hurdle. We finally got clearance from the INS and all required paperwork for our dossier was ready to be sent to Romania. Then we learned of an additional process that some countries, including Romania, require, where your documents must be verified for authenticity. This process is called "Apostilizing." So again our dossier had to go through another slow and expensive pro-cess.

After our dossier was "apostillized" it was certified in Washington, D.C. and then finally ready to go to Romania. Yet another setback occurred. While reviewing our dossier one last time before sending it to Romania, Radu found an error on Gregg's passport. His last name was spelled wrong; we have two "n's" on the end of Rietmann and they had only put one. How we didn't notice it before is beyond me. So off the passport had to go to be corrected.

Every setback seemed like it took an eternity to deal with. It seemed like it was one thing after another. During the time we were waiting for our dossier to be completed we received a phone call from Radu. He called to ask if we would consider twins? Thinking we had thought everything through, this really was a curve ball. It was a spring afternoon and Gregg was working in the shop. We had never talked about twins or getting two children, so I told Radu we'd talk about it and get back to him.

I almost didn't even consider it. I mean, twins were a bit more than we bargained for. I walked out to the shop to "throw" this prospect at Gregg. I told him to give it some thought and we'd talk tonight. As I was walking away Gregg said, "I don't need to think about it; I thing it would be great!" Rather surprised, I stopped, turned around, and stared at him in disbelief. "Really?" I said. "You really think we can handle this?" "It would be a lot more on you," Gregg said, "so ultimately it needs to be your decision. But I'm all for it?"

I actually couldn't believe we were considering this. When the terror subsided and I was able to give it careful consideration, I started to think that maybe we might be able to handle it. I called Radu and asked if he had a picture he could e-mail us and he did. When the picture of the twins came up on the screen of course my heart melted. Tears came immediately to my eyes and a lump in my throat grew so big I could hardly swallow.

They were so beautiful. It was a boy and a girl. Their names were Alexandra and Alexandru. I ran out to the shop and told Gregg he needed to come look at these twins. All we could say was "Wow!" We talked about all the pros and cons. We thought about how wonderful it would be that they would have each other to play with. We thought about the connection twins have with one another. Would two really be that much harder than one?

We called Radu back the next day and said we would take them. I immediately started forwarding their picture to family and friends. At that time Radu was pretty sure we would get the twins. Romania was full of political problems. Adoption there had become a mess and Romania and the U.S. were working through mounds of propaganda. The twins were considered to be "special needs" since there were two of them and they were over a year old, so they were supposed to be "released" soon despite all the political problems.

My apprehension about the prospect of twins soon turned to excitement. When the boys got home from school that night we showed them the pictures and they were even more excited than Gregg and me. Being assured by Radu that we would eventually get these twins, I began preparing. I started getting their room ready and showing everyone their pictures. I looked at their picture ten times a day.

We agreed we would call Alexandru, "Dru", and Alexandra, "Lexi". I really embraced the idea that two would not be that much harder than one. Evan thought it would be so cool to "have" a younger brother rather having to "be" the younger brother. He said many times that "HE would be nice to his little brother" (apparently his point being that HIS older brother is NOT nice to him!).

We enjoyed many long discussions about the twins. We were amazed but we really did decide to "go for it." We felt that if this was the road God had led us down that he would provide us with the help we'd need to do this. We would welcome not one, but two little ones who needed us.

We were so excited when our dossier finally made it to Romania. The INS wired our visas to Romania also. Now the waiting really became painful! Now I actually had a picture of my kids in my head and in my heart. We had an intense and overwhelming need to get to them and bring them home. The days went by and then months and no good news. Radu kept assuring us they would be released soon. He told us to write letters to the Secretary of State in Romania, which we did immediately. Even the boys wrote letters pleading for them to release these special needs orphans.

It is so heart breaking to see the pictures of these precious little children who desperately need homes, and watch them become "political pawns." But that is exactly what happens, unfortunately. We felt so helpless. So many children need homes and there are so many homes waiting for them. Politicians block the adoption process because of bitterness and hatred for one country or another. They actually use them for leverage and bartering on other issues. There is a lot of pride within these countries, not just in Romania, but with most countries that are involved in international adoption. Their goal is to keep their own children in their own countries.

This is understandable, but not realistic. Many of these countries, mostly because of poverty, are unable to find homes for these children. There are more orphans than available homes within their countries. The sad thing is that so many of these children could be in homes rather than in orphanages or foster care if these countries could find it in their hearts to put aside their differences, ease regulations, and allow these children to be adopted.

Along with all the political problems there is also a lot of corruption and "black marketing" going on. Children, especially babies, are basically sold to the highest bidder. This leads to foreign adoptions in these countries getting shut down. It is really heart breaking.

After many months of waiting we finally made the heart-wrenching decision to leave the Romanian program and our precious little twins behind. We had waited a long time and there seemed to be no promise of them being released anytime soon. We felt we had no choice other than to switch to a different country to adopt. It was a really hard process giving up Romania and the twins. We felt like we were abandoning Lexi and Dru. They had been "our babies" in our hearts for months now. Surprisingly, I think it was hardest on Gregg.

5

"Carried on Angel's wings"

We swallowed our tears and moved forward. We had to let go and choose another country. We eventually settled on the Ukraine. We chose the Ukraine for many reasons, one of them being that you were required to travel to that country only one time. The amount of time we might have to stay there was "unsure" but we would hope for the best. The children we saw from there were of course beautiful and we were really intrigued by the Ukrainian people and their country. We did a lot of reading and found the Ukrainians to be very strong, independent, resourceful, and artistic people. This small country had fought hard and surprisingly had won its fight to be independent.

By now it had been over a year since our dossier was completed and we had to update many of our documents. I became disheartened during this time. The process was taking so much longer than we thought. I did not understand why we seemed to be having so many setbacks. I wondered if God was trying to tell me something. Maybe we were not meant to adopt after all; maybe he had another plan for us, something different we were supposed to be doing. I prayed lots of prayers and cried lots of tears.

At the beginning of our adoption process, I had a conversation with one of my best friends about our decision to adopt. My friend Lea and I had talked many times about adopting, as she too had always wanted to adopt. When she learned we were really going to do it, she reacted enthusiastically by saying, "OK, if you can do it so can we!"

I was excited that we would be doing this together. Lea and her husband's process went a little smoother than ours. As she has said, "it was a straight line" for them. Lea and her husband, Joel, have two biological boys also, so they too decided to adopt a little girl. Their journey led them to India. Lea and Joel had a long, painful waiting period also but a little "smoother" and less confusing. They found their little girl right away through Holtz Adoption Agency. Lea knew immediately after reading her biography that this was her daughter. They had to work through the long and tedious paperwork required by the Indian government. At least they knew where their daughter was though.

It took them about a year, but they were successful in getting to her and bringing her home. When they brought Babali home from India we were so happy for them. Babali is a beautiful, vivacious little girl whom everyone fell in love with immediately! It was obvious to everyone, including Babali, that she was exactly where she was supposed to be. Very little adjustment was needed for this bright little girl to thrive heartily in her new home.

Although I was so, so happy for them, it was bittersweet for me. They had started their adoption months after we did. I kept thinking, "We must be doing something wrong!" They had managed to find their daughter and get her home. Why couldn't we do that? Something made us "hang in there" though. Again, surprisingly, whenever I wanted to quit, Gregg was the one to push us on. Somewhere in the process, even though I was the one who originally started the idea of adopting, many times Gregg was the one who kept us going. Gregg would be the one to say, "There's a little girl waiting for us and we can't give up."

I'm grateful for Gregg's strength and perseverance. I'm glad we kept going as it was so worth it in the end. After we got through the "grieving process" over the twins, we pulled ourselves together and moved excitedly into the Ukrainian program. First we had to request our dossier back from Romania. We sent a letter doing so. Next we had to contact the INS and have our visas rewired to the Ukraine. Of course, all this took an excruciating amount of time.

In the middle of all the changes we had to make with switching countries our agency and our social worker, Radu, had a "falling out" and decided to "part ways." This was a difficult transition for us and we felt a little caught in the middle. It was like being the children in the middle of a divorce. We were talking both with Radu and our agency, Journeys of the Heart. At times we got conflicting information. Our "base" in our adoption process felt a little shaky. We weren't sure who we should be taking advice from now, Radu or our agency.

Radu was very hurt and angry with our agency and we felt the friction. Everything worked out fine in the end, but this was just one more upset in our story and added to our frustration.

The first thing that needs to happen when you're in the Ukrainian adoption program is getting an appointment with the National Adoption Center in Kiev. Our adoption agency sent a letter to the center requesting an appointment. This takes anywhere from sixty to ninety days from the time you send a request to the time you actually get an appointment. It doesn't help that this is all done by mail, which is very slow in the Ukraine. Again, the waiting and the waiting! Families during this time prepare to travel. You are usually only given a week or two notice of your appointment date, so you have to be ready to go with last-minute travel arrangements. Radu and our agency have a very competent attorney in the Ukraine. Your attorney/facilitator can make all the difference in your adoption experience in a foreign country.

Our attorney's name was Yuri. Yuri definitely knows his way around the National Adoption Center and how the adoption process works in the Ukraine. He seems to be in good standing with the Adoption Center and this helped a lot. Yuri knew first when we finally had been given an appointment at the National Adoption Center. Radu phoned us with the good news. Susan, at Journeys of the Heart, called later in the day to also give us the news. Susan was so disappointed that she didn't get to be the first to tell us the good news. In any case it was great news and I jumped up and down with excitement and cried at the same time. This was it! I was working at a friend's coffee shop that day and had given Radu the phone number there. I shared the news with everyone who came into the coffee shop that day and ran all over town telling everyone, "We are finally going to get out little girl." Everyone knew how long we had been waiting and they were happy for us.

We had less than a week to make travel arrangements. We would fly out on May 31, 2004, which was Memorial Day. We were so excited and also scared to death. We began communicating with Yuri on a regular basis now. Yuri needed to know what we were hoping for as far as the child we would like to adopt. We told him we hoped to find a "healthy" baby girl between the age of one and three.

Yuri's response was, "There are no healthy children in the Ukraine." He told us he would do his best to help us though. This was bit unsettling to hear from our attorney, but we still stayed positive. I did tons of research on the Internet and used every available media source I had to prepare for our journey. For every little bit of positive information I'd find on the adoption process in the Ukraine there would be the same amount of horror stories.

After riding on the roller coaster of emotional ups and downs we finally decided to quit reading anything on adopting in the Ukraine. We were ready, come what may. I sent an emotional e-mail to friends and family asking for their prayers and telling them to prepare for anything, as we were very unsure what would happen. I shared all my hopes and fears. We might come home with a "perfect" little girl, or maybe a little boy it that's where we were lead! Our child could have some medical problems and likely would be somewhat "delayed." We might not come home with a child at all. All these things and more had happened to many families. These are the things they prepared us for. I felt the need to prepare our family and friends for these possibilities also. We were going to need all the support we could get.

I solicited advice on the Internet from others who had traveled to the Ukraine, on how to pack. Everyone said it would most likely be cold. I also kept hearing that I should dress very casual and in dark colors so as not to stand out. Everyone kept saying that we should not come across as "flashy" Americans. We received some helpful information that we were grateful for, but we also received a lot of false information that we laughed about later.

Preparing to leave the boys was the hardest part of our preparation. The Ukrainian government has a standard thirty-day waiting period after you've found your child and petitioned to adopt. We were told that in some cases the 30 day waiting period was waived, but that recently they were seeing it waived less and less. We of course prayed that our thirty days would be waived. If it wasn't waived, it would be devastating to have to leave our new baby behind in the Ukraine, but we couldn't imagine being away from our boys for thirty days either.

We had to be prepared to possibly be gone thirty days or make more than one trip. The cost of traveling, lodging, food, etc., would affect our decision. If after finding our child and petitioning to adopt we were not able to get the thirty-day waiting period waived, we would then have to decide whether one or both of us would stay in the Ukraine, or whether we'd come back home and return in thirty days. Either way it would be emotionally and financially very difficult.

We decided to take it one day at a time and cross each bridge as we came to it. If you try to take on the whole picture all at once it's just too overwhelming! There were still so many "unknowns" ahead. We began packing and making arrangements for the boys, the farm, etc. Basically, we would need people to step in and "take over our lives." We tried to leave instructions behind for "worst case scenarios." It was difficult thinking about those things but we knew we needed to have all our affairs in order. While looking over our wills and other legal documents one afternoon Gregg said to me, "Shelly I know you want to be cremated when you die, but you've never told me where you want your ashes scattered"? As I contemplated this, Gregg, trying to be helpful added; "Well, where is your favorite place in the world?" I immediately responded with; "You can't spread my ashes in the Nordstrom's shoe department!" This helped lighten the moment a bit!

Later, Gregg would share with me how scared he really was. He was sure we would be robbed and murdered in the Ukraine. So we took care of all the "just in case" things and felt ready to go. We are so fortunate to have such wonderful family, friends, and neighbors. Everyone came forward in the most amazing ways. After 9/11 and with all the terrorist alerts, traveling to another country is a lot scarier than it used to be. I don't think I realized how worried everyone was for us until later. I was just worried about finding our little girl and that was really all I thought about.

Gregg worried about everything else! We tried to remain positive, and we were for the most part. My good friend Stacie would become our main point of contact, as telephoning would be difficult. Our cell phones would not work there so we weren't sure until we got there how we would call home. We would make sure that Stacie always knew where we were and also where the boys were at all times. Stacie would make sure everyone else was kept informed of our progress also. God love her for doing this for us, as it wasn't always an easy task! She and her husband and daughter stayed at our house a lot so that the boys' lives weren't too interrupted. We also hired a college girl to come stay with them after school was out. School would be getting out for the summer about a week after we left.

My mom and my sisters were always there to help with the boys too. They kept them busy and made sure they were ok emotionally. We hired help to mow the lawn, water plants, drive the tractor, feed the animals, and get things done on the farm. We had no problem finding people willing to help out. Everyone was there with words of encouragement and lots of prayers.

Adrienne sent the most beautiful e-mail, saying how she knew from experience how wonderful it could be to be adopted into such a loving family and how lucky this little girl would be. Even though each e-mail and phone call made me cry before we left, we drew an enormous amount of strength from each and every one of them.

By the time we left we had little concern that everything would be well taken care of at home while we were gone. Our only real concern was how long we would have to be gone. I couldn't let myself think too much about how long I might have to be away from my boys. We hadn't been away from them much more than a rare three-day weekend, so this was going to be really tough on all of us.

Saying good-bye at the airport was very hard. I kept saying, "Don't cry, don't cry, don't cry." (Of course, I cried.) My mom was there and helped greatly by offering to buy new video games for the boys, which proved to be a brilliant distraction. She managed to get them out the door and headed for the mall before we all fell apart.

6

"Finally on our way!"

Getting on the plane I was feeling so many emotions. As I said before, there were so many unknowns ahead. I was scared, excited, nervous, and happy. We had waited so long and we were finally going to get our daughter. We flew from Pasco to Seattle, and then from Seattle to Amsterdam.

We sat by a family from Alaska. The wife/mother was from Sweden, and they were on their way to visit her family there. They had an adorable little girl, three, and a little boy, eight months. They were wonderful to visit with. I think I told everyone who even glanced my way that we were on our way to the Ukraine to adopt a little girl. There was no containing my excitement.

The family we sat by was great fun to talk with. They were very loving, friendly, and interesting. Listening to them talk about their family in Sweden and their family in Seattle, and all the places they had traveled to, made me realize how small the world really is and how connected we all are. I love when people come together from different parts of the world to form families and friendships. This is how it is meant to be. Their little girl drew me a picture and gave it to me. I told her I would give it to my little girl someday. I still have it and will keep my promise. She smiled the biggest smile. She was so cute. Her name was Sarafina; it was a family name we were told. (Later I would think of the coincidence it was that my daughter's family name was Saragina, very close to Sarafina!) I kept looking at this sweet little girl and thinking, "I'm going to have a daughter too!"

It was amazing to me how much everyone on our airplane, total strangers, seemed to have encouraging words and good wishes. We started hearing all these wonderful stories about adoption. The family we sat by made the time go by fast. I held their little boy and played with Sarafina. They said at the end of our flight "what a blessing it was to sit by us," and we felt the same way about them. As anyone who's traveled with children knows, it can be very difficult. You find out quickly those who like children and those who don't. I've decided I don't like people who don't like children!

On the trip over I honestly felt we were being carried on angels' wings. I saw only love and kindness all around me. Everyone was smiling, their eyes filled with affirmation. The world suddenly felt small and I felt connected to the entire universe! I sat by an elderly lady who I guessed had to have been from the Middle East somewhere. I could tell just by looking at her that she had not had an easy life. She had apparently been visiting family in the Seattle area. I couldn't help but think how very different our lives probably were. As I studied her tired body and the signs of aging and hard work in her eyes, I glanced down and saw that she had on the same shoes as me! We had on the same black sandals from Payless Shoes. I smiled, thinking again how much more we are alike than different. Those who know me well, would not be surprised that I connect many of life's "deep and meaningful" moments to "shoes"!

We had a short layover in Amsterdam, where we had a couple of beers in a cute pub at the airport. I wish we could have done a little sightseeing there as it looked like a beautiful place from the window. We were on an important mission now though, with no time for sightseeing! In a couple of hours we were back on our plane and off to Kiev. We were getting closer, only a few more hours to the Ukraine. When we landed in Kiev, after traveling twenty-one hours, the time change had me completely confused on what time it was or even what day it was! I just knew I was very tired and looking forward to a bed and getting some sleep.

When we got off the plane it was early afternoon. Yuri had arranged for his personal driver, Jenya, to pick us up at the airport. Jenya was waiting for us, holding a sign saying Rietmann. We quickly learned about the "very loud disco" type music that they play everywhere in the Ukraine. The minute we got off the plane it started, very loud disco music. I do mean EVERYWHERE you go, very LOUD disco music.

Driving into Kiev the city looked very clean and basically like any other large city you might visit anywhere. As you get more into the city, however, you realize the contrast between the very rich and the very poor. Not a lot in between. The traffic is crazy. Everyone drives very fast. No one uses their blinkers and they change lanes often and quickly. We were scared to death! Jenya's car was old and beat up, as were most of the cars we saw there. Again there was a big contrast, very nice cars or very old beat up cars. On our way to meet Yuri, Jenya's car overheated and we had to pull off the road to let it cool. "It happens often," Jenya told us! We were very nervous! We had been in the Ukraine for less than an hour and here we were sitting alongside the highway in an old broken down car with smoke coming out of the hood! Not the most reassuring way to start out.

We finally made it to Yuri's office building. Yuri came down to the parking lot to meet us. Yuri looked so different than I had him pictured in my mind. He was young (probably twenty-eight or so). He had blond hair with long bangs that "swept" down into his eyes. He was dressed in a very nice suit with shiny, pointed black shoes. Very "debonair," I thought. He smoked one cigarette after another. It had been suggested to us that we take our attorney in the Ukraine a gift. It was "customary" to do this. Something for him and his family would be nice, we were told. We had been given some suggestions, cigarettes for Yuri, some perfume for his wife, and an outfit for his little daughter. We gave him these gifts and thanked him in advance for the help he would be giving us. He asked if we'd prefer to stay in a hotel or an apartment. We decided to take the apartment for the first night, as it was actually cheaper than the hotel. Our appointment with the National Adoption Center was the next morning and we would know more about where we'd be going and could make longer term lodging arrangements after that.

The streets in the center of Kiev were very clean; outside the city limits it's a different story. The historical monuments and statues were amazing. There is so much history there that dates back hundreds, even thousands of years. The weather was sunny and beautiful. Yuri finished with us regarding our business details and he then had Jenya take us to our apartment building. Yuri made sure we had his number and told us to get a good night's sleep so we would be ready to go to the Adoption Center first thing in the morning. Our appointment was at 9:00 a.m.

We had read many times that it was better to get an early morning appointment with the National Adoption Center, so we were pleased. When we pulled up to our apartment building we thought it looked very old but nice enough. We unloaded and once inside the building, we got into the elevator as our apartment was on the eighth floor. The elevator was positively antique. I thought it looked like something you might see in a grain elevator. It was small and pitch black inside. Gregg, Jenya, myself, and our luggage were crammed into this tiny, dark elevator. I had really tried to pack light but as anyone who knows me knows, I'm just not capable of packing light, so we had a very large suitcase. We pushed the button and heard a lot of loud, banging, clanging, and grinding. We went up a few floors and with some more loud banging and clanging, we came to an abrupt halt. We waited for the door to open. Nothing happened. In total darkness, we found the buttons and pressed them all, hoping the door would open or we'd go to the next floor. Nothing happened! We frantically pressed them again and again. Nothing happened! Gregg went into total panic. I, for some reason, stayed calm. I refused to believe that we had gone through all this to end up dying in an elevator in Kiev.

After what seemed like an eternity, and with Gregg hyperventilating, the elevator started to work again, and we did make it to our floor and into our apartment. Even though we were on the eighth floor, we never again got in that elevator.

Our apartment was decorated in 1920's art deco animal print. It was quite interesting. It was spacious, open, and sunny though. It had a bed to sleep in, which was all we cared about.

We had been told ahead of time that the water there was "gross" and this proved to be quite true. It was brown and stunk terribly. We had some bottled water, which we drank and washed our faces with. We had a terrible time buying bottled water there, as most Ukrainians drink seltzer water, which we were not used to, and it just didn't quench our thirst. It was very hard to find regular drinking or spring water like we buy here.

Eventually, we fell into bed for a nap. When we woke after a few hours we felt refreshed enough to venture out. It was late afternoon. The first thing we wanted to do was buy a cell phone. The phone in our apartment didn't work and our cell phones didn't work either. We tried and failed to use the pay phones. We couldn't even get in touch with Yuri, which made us very nervous. We had no way to communicate with anyone and it was difficult to find anyone who spoke English. This was when it hit us. "Hey, we're in a foreign country where we don't speak the language." You don't realize how frightening these sorts of things are until you are actually experiencing them for yourselves.

We made our way around downtown and luckily we found a large store that sold cell phones nearby. There was one person at the store who spoke a little English. We managed to purchase a cell phone and plenty of minutes. This made us feel a lot better and more secure. We made sure Yuri had our new cell phone number and later gave it to family and friends back home. We would come to cherish that cell phone as it kept us in touch with home and also with Yuri. We felt much safer having that "life line" for communication.

We were hungry for dinner so we began to look around for somewhere to eat. Again we realized we were in a foreign country where we didn't speak the language. How would we order food or drinks when we couldn't read the menu? When we tried to order in English, they would sometimes nod as if they understood, but then we would seldom get what we thought we had actually ordered! Gregg can eat anything, but I am not comfortable eating something if I have no idea what it is.

We found a little French restaurant in a fairly modern hotel. We didn't realize until later that that would be the last familiar style meal we would have for a while. Who knew a Caesar salad, ice water, and a glass of Chardonnay could be so wonderful.

We slept well that night even though we were nervous and excited about the next day. We woke very early, about 4:00 a.m. Ukrainian time. We couldn't wait for our appointment. This was the day we had waited so long for. It was possible that we would see our daughter for the first time on this day! Yuri told us that after we found a child in the books at the NAC that we would probably be able to visit the orphanage the same day.

We got up and started getting ready. We couldn't make the coffee pot work, but that was OK since I would have had to make it with the brown, barely drizzling water. We weren't sure if we could drink it anyway. We had one tiny towel in the whole entire apartment to bathe and dry off with. We tried to wait calmly for 8:00 to roll around but we were too nervous to just sit there. It's funny how you don't realize how much you enjoy your routines at home, like drinking your coffee, reading the paper, or watching the morning news; we had none of these luxuries here now!

Gregg and I sat nervously staring at each other until I said, "OK, let's go try to find some coffee." As we stepped out into the streets we first began to realize that Kiev is definitely populated by "night owls." NO ONE is up at 7:00 a.m. We walked around anyway. It was a beautiful morning, sunny and warm. There was a man standing on a street corner with a huge, gorgeous white owl. He had a camera and offered to take a picture of us with his owl for twenty dollars. On the next street corner was a man with a monkey, offering to take a picture for twenty dollars. Slowly, more and more street vendors appeared with their wares, flowers, fruits, vegetables, artwork, tee shirts, and more.

We found a nice hotel with a restaurant that advertised breakfast so we headed in. As we were waiting for the restaurant to open we noticed a man in the lobby who was also waiting. He overheard us talking in English and asked where we were from. We told him, and he said he too was from the United States. We told him we were in the Ukraine to adopt, and to our amazement he owned and operated an adoption agency in Michigan. He was there to facilitate an adoption. He invited us to join him for breakfast and we eagerly accepted. We felt so fortunate to find this nice gentleman who offered us so much encouragement and good advice. We enjoyed our breakfast with him so much, and once again marveled at how small the world really is! I had read about and even considered his adoption agency on the Internet. It is called All God's Children.

We went back to our apartment and nervously waited for Yuri to call. The minutes ticked by slowly. Finally, Yuri phoned and told us that Jenya would be by soon to pick us up and to wait for him outside in front of our building. Jenya showed up and we jumped in with him, excited to be heading for the National Adoption Center. The roads within the city are narrow and crooked. Again, we were terrified at how fast everyone drives. This didn't help our already high anxiety level on the way to the NAC. I was digging my nails into Gregg's leg the whole time. Wide-eyed, we clung to each other.

When we pulled up to the building where the National Adoption Center was I was amazed at how old and rundown it looked. I thought, "This is the place we waited so long to get clearance to visit? This is the place where thousands of children's futures are determined?" We would soon realize that all the government buildings were very old and rundown and not very clean.

I could hardly breathe, I was so nervous. Everyone told us to be very polite, as it could make a big difference in how we were treated. I was so glad to be there early in the morning, as there were not many people there yet. We had heard stories of people waiting hours. We were told that often people would be standing in the hallways waiting and waiting and then sometimes being turned away. Yuri told us to wait in the waiting room while he went in to talk with the director first. It wasn't long until he came back to get us. We went down a long hallway to the director's office. There were pictures of children, orphanages, and families who had adopted all along the walls. My heart pounded. The director was also much younger than I expected. She was very pretty and nice. She and Yuri seemed well-acquainted and were talking back and forth in Ukrainian.

You start to get sort of paranoid when everyone is talking a different language. You begin to think they are talking about you. I'm sure they were not, but that's how you feel sometimes.

Three large, old notebooks were plopped down in front of us. These were the books we had to go through, full of photos of adoptable children. We had tried to prepare for this, but it was overwhelming. How do you find "your child" in these huge books? You pray for guidance from above, and hope that maybe, somehow, you will just know which child is meant to be yours.

It was more terrifying than we ever could have imagined. All those precious little faces looking up at us on every page. The lump in my throat grew bigger. They all looked so scared and alone. How could we possibly choose? Gregg sat behind me in a trance, looking to me for guidance, and me looking back at him for some input.

I asked about a few different children and each child I chose had severe medical problems. Many had hepatitis or AIDS. Many had severe vision problems. Many were either retarded or severely handicapped. I kept turning the pages. I thought I was either going to cry or throw up. This was absolutely the hardest thing I had ever done in my life. I began praying! "Please God, help us." As I said before, I was completely overwhelmed! Yuri and the director were chatting back and forth all this time (almost in a "flirtatious" manner), seemingly unaware of the trauma Gregg and I were experiencing. I would ask a question about one of the children and one of them would answer and then go back to chatting in Ukrainian.

We had spent about thirty minutes going through the books, and had not been able to find a child without serious problems. The director got up, went to a cabinet, and pulled out a piece of paper. The paper had information on a child who had not been put in the books yet. The director seemed mildly annoyed and set the paper down in front of us. With Yuri translating, she told us that this was a "healthy baby girl just released today." While we were reading the paper, Yuri said, "you will not find a child healthier than this one. You should go and see her."

We mustered some enthusiasm and numbly agreed. The picture was of a baby swaddled in a blanket. You could barely see her face and the picture was at least a year old. We really couldn't tell what she looked like. Again, Yuri said, "You will not do better than this." We agreed in hopes that God had intervened and that this was our little girl. Her name, they said, was Kryla Olga Sergina. "Sign here, sign here, sign here, and you're off!" We weren't sure how we felt at this point, but again "faith and guidance" from somewhere told us we were on the right path. We stumbled out into the hallway, waiting to be told what to do next. Thinking we were leaving, the director came back out into the hallway and asked Yuri to come back into her office. He asked us to wait while he, the director, and another attorney went back into her office and closed the door. Something seemed to be wrong. We could hear some "arguing" going on in the director's office. We sat barely breathing. Across from us sat another couple who seemed to be glaring at us. They were an older, hefty, very stern-looking couple dressed in expensive clothing and jewelry. Obviously quite wealthy. We were nervous and had no idea what was going on. After much yelling and commotion, which we could hear out in the hallway, Yuri finally came out and said discreetly, "We are done here; follow me. I have taken care of everything, but do not act too happy."

Completely confused about what was happening, and "not looking too happy," we followed Yuri outside. Yuri was not smiling! When we were in the car Yuri explained to us that the child we were going to meet had been promised illegally to the couple sitting across from us at the NAC. They were, in fact, a very wealthy couple from Israel. It is illegal in the Ukraine to "arrange" adoptions prior to going through the NAC. Apparently, the attorney involved was not successful in what appeared to be a scam on his part and he was told he must go through the "proper channels" required by the Ukrainian government as we had done.

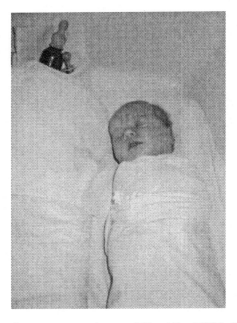

First picture we were shown of Ola at the NAC in Kiev

Although they may have been very nice people, we cannot help but believe that Olga was meant to be with us. We were glad we had done everything the "right way" and grateful that we seemed to have a good attorney and adoption facilitator in Yuri. Yuri then explained to us that our little girl was in an orphanage in a city called Zaporizhia. We would need to get on a train and travel for about twelve hours. If Yuri was able to make all the arrangements, we would board our train at 6:00 that evening and arrive in Zaporizhia at about 6:00 a.m. the next morning.

Yuri took us back to our apartment and told us to begin packing our belongings and prepare to travel again. Before leaving he told us if all went well he would send Jenya to pick us up and take us to the train station in a few hours. He told us he would call soon. We packed quickly and decided to walk around the square close by with our cell phone in hand waiting for Yuri to call. In Kiev they have underground tunnels that go underneath the roads above. This is probably good considering the way people drive. The way people drive there I would imagine crossing the road could be very danger-ous. I was nervous in the underground. It was dark, crowded, and no one smiled.

There were vendors everywhere selling all kinds of wares but they were not friendly. We learned that it is considered "bad luck" to have your picture taken underground. Gregg tried to take some pictures and at first was just given dirty looks; then a large man jumped out and shook his finger, scolding Gregg. We were quite puzzled. When Gregg tried to snap photos, people hid, mothers grabbed and shel-tered their children behind them. We quit taking pictures in the underground tunnels. Yuri later told us that indeed, it was definitely considered very bad luck to have your picture taken underground!

When we got to the other side, we bought a few souvenirs at the open square and headed back to our apartment. We were anxious for Yuri to call and hoping we would be heading to Zaporizhia that night. Luckily Yuri was able to make all the arrangements. He told us another attorney would be meeting us at the train station and accom-panying us to Zaporizhia. He also told us this attorney was "very good at dealing with adoptions in difficult regions." This, of course, made us nervous. Apparently, we were going to a difficult region. Again, we loaded up in Jenya's car for another scary ride. Fast and furious we made it to the train station.

At the train station, once again, very loud disco music was playing everywhere! Yuri had told us there would be a place we could check some of our luggage at the train station. He advised us to take only what we could carry comfortably to Zaporizhia. We would be "on the run a lot in Zaporizhia" and he was "not sure where we would be staying." So taking his advice, we left some of our belongings in the Kiev train station. Now that we realized how warm it was in the Ukraine this time of year, we were happy to leave some of our heavy coats and sweatshirts!

The attorney that would be going to Zaporizhia with us met us at the train station. Her name was "Luba." Luba was a tall, sturdy, but attractive lady. She spoke little English. She had arranged for two interpreters to meet us in Zaporizhia. Our interpreters would help us communicate with Luba and everyone else we would need to communicate with there.

The train ride with Luba proved to be very interesting and difficult. Not speaking the same language, we tried to have dinner and visit in the dining car. The train was loud, clankity, and very bumpy. Rocking back and forth, we spent a lot of time smiling and politely nodding at one another. We often would start out trying to convey something to Luba and her with us and eventually, frustrated and embarrassed, we would have to give up. I ordered chicken for dinner and got steak. Potatoes everywhere there are usually "pureed" (not mashed, but pureed, like baby food) but very good. I ordered white wine and got red.

We really didn't care what we ate or drank. We were so excited to be on our way to meet our daughter. I kept thinking to myself, tomorrow I will be meeting my daughter! Before it got dark we looked out the windows. We went through miles and miles of farmland. The soil looked dark and rich and the fields very green. We didn't go through any large towns to speak of, a few small communities, but mostly just miles of farmland. None of the farmhouses had yards with grass; their homes were surrounded by huge vegetable and herb gardens. Homes in the Ukraine seemed not to be for "show" but all about "survival." Not a single square inch of soil is wasted in the Ukraine. Nothing is used for landscaping. Any and all "dirt" is used to grow something to eat or sell. The homes, barns, and outbuildings were all very old and barely standing, but obviously still in use. The countryside was very beautiful though. Much more beautiful than the cities we would visit! We finally settled into our sleeping compartment for the night. I took my Exedrine PM, put my earplugs in, and tried to get some sleep. The train was cold and rickety. Not only could I hear my husband snoring but all the others who were snoring on the train. Cold and skeptical of the possibility I would be able to sleep, I prayed until I drifted off.

We awoke as soon as the sun was shining, probably around 5:00 in the morning. We waited in line for the bathroom. We were given a washrag and a towel (no soap)! We freshened up as best we could. I made my way down the shaky, cold, and dark aisle to the café car to see if I could find a cup of coffee. Some of the kitchen crew were sleeping in the booths of the tables in their work clothes. They seemed very annoyed that I was bothering them so I made my way back to our sleeping car without coffee.

Coffee in the Ukraine is what we would consider espresso here in the U.S. Apparently most Europeans drink espresso with lots of sugar or chocolate. We were grateful for the espresso, but longed for our old familiar Starbucks. Luba came to our sleeping car to check on us and tell us we should be arriving soon in Zaporizhia. Once again we sat anxiously waiting and trying to communicate with Luba.

7

"Meeting Ola"

When we pulled into Zaporizhia, once again the loud disco music was blaring away. The train station reminded me of something out of an old German movie. Everything was old, rundown, and dirty.

We gathered our things and got off the train. Luba began looking for a taxi. Taxis don't look like the taxis that we are used to. They are old beat-up cars that you would never in a million years get into here. The cars are often not marked "Taxi," so I wondered how you even knew who was really a taxi driver? The taxi drivers there scared me. They ranged from older gentlemen in old dirty suits to young boys with ripped t-shirts and tattoos! I hoped and prayed Gregg's fear that we'd be taken to the middle of nowhere, robbed, and murdered would not come true. Luba did not seem concerned at all. We headed back behind the station and Luba called to one of the men who apparently was a taxi driver and we piled into a rickety old car and off we flew! Luba gave directions to the driver on where we needed to go. Once again, as in Kiev, Zaporizhia would go from a very nice area with beautiful old historical buildings and very clean surroundings, to absolute poverty and filth.

We stopped at one hotel, that looked very nice, clean, secluded, and surrounded by trees. We waited while Luba went in. Apparently, they had no rooms available. Away we went into the more central downtown part of Zaporizhia. We came to a hotel called Hotel Intourist. Luba said that this would be a good place for us to stay as it catered to Westerners. (Later I would think it was more like they "tolerated" us rather than "catered" to us!) Everywhere you go in the Ukraine it is like going back in time. The Hotel Intourist is considered to be one of the more modern hotels, but it felt like we were back in the fifties at best. They did have a one-hour photo shop and e-mailing capabilities. This would become a "huge deal" to Gregg and me as it was an ongoing, cost effective connection to home.

It was so much fun to e-mail pictures home, and the e-mails we received back from family and friends truly kept us going. It became our favorite part of the day when we would send and receive e-mails to and from home. I would cry every single time I sat down to write and read e-mails.

The rooms were very small and we had trouble getting a room with a double bed. We were shown two rooms with one or two single beds, which Gregg and I were fine with, but Luba kept telling them, "they married; one double bed!" We finally got a room and checked in. Luba said to rest a bit and get ready to go to the Ministry of Education, where we would need to receive clearance to visit the orphanage. We had about an hour to freshen up and grab some breakfast.

We took quick showers and went looking for the restaurant. On the top floor we found a breakfast buffet for guests. There was juice, sweet rolls, spicy dried meats, hard-boiled eggs, and yogurt. I never knew how much I loved yogurt until we visited the Ukraine. It became a staple for me, as it was one of the few things I could eat. Gregg loved the spicy, greasy meats, cheese, and rolls, but they were too rich and greasy for me, especially first thing in the morning. They did have "American" style coffee, which made us happy.

We met with Luba in the lobby and we were introduced to our interpreters for the first time. They were two teachers from the university there who could speak English. Their names were Natasha and Yanna. They were both beautiful girls. They were tall and thin with long dark hair and dark eyes. The women in the Ukraine, along with being very beautiful (especially the young ones), dress very "provocatively." They wear pointed-toed stiletto style shoes, very tight pants, dresses, or skirts. Their tops are almost always cropped and very sheer, leaving little to the imagination. They all had flawless figures, wore makeup, and bright lipstick. Poor Gregg got "elbowed" many times for staring (mouth slightly open and drooling)! I felt "frumpy" the whole time I was there! I cursed the people who had told me to dress in dark, drab clothes so as not to stand out.

Never being able to get my hair dryer or curling iron to work, I wore my hair in a pony tail the whole time and there was no time for makeup. It was also very warm and humid there. As I mentioned before, we had been misled about the weather at this time of year and had packed heavy clothing. At one point in our trip we decided we needed to buy a couple pair of shorts and some lightweight shirts so we went shopping. I especially had a hard time finding any clothes that I felt comfortable in, as all the women's clothes there are so tiny and revealing. Also, they were very flashy, brightly colored usually with sequins.

Gregg and I finally found a store that had "sporty" clothing that we felt we might be comfortable in. We were able to buy a few things there. It was funny because the salesperson said to us (very proudly), "This is USA clothing line!" We had already figured this out. We had come all this way and ended up buying "Columbia Sportswear," made in Portland, Oregon.

After introductions all five of us piled into a teeny, tiny cab, Yanna sat on Natasha's lap, and I sat on Gregg's lap, and off we went to the Department of Ministry and Education. Seatbelts are unheard of there. We got there about 9:00 a.m. and it was not open yet. As I mentioned before, everyone in the Ukraine stays up late and gets up late! Nothing opens early; the restaurants, the shops, even government offices open about 10:00 or 11:00. The city does not come alive until around 11:00 a.m. We did, however, find a little Irish-style pub that happened to be open and they let us come in for coffee and tea. We hung out there for about an hour.

It was fun to visit with and get to know Natasha, Yanna, and Luba. Finally, with the help of our interpreters we could talk to Luba.

We could ask each other questions and Natasha and Yanna would interpret back and forth. Natasha, Yanna, and I "bonded" immediately. They were the sweetest girls. We established the basics of why we were there and our hopes of adopting a little girl.

With Natasha and Yanna interpreting we were able to find out and prepare for what would be happening next. Luba told us how she hoped the rest of the day would go. We would need first to get clearance from the Department of Ministry and Education. If all went well we would get some sort of "stamp" of approval that we would then need to have notarized along with all our other paperwork. With this paperwork in hand we would then be able to visit the orphanage. After meeting with the orphanage's director and getting her OK we could then meet Olga.

We were so nervous and excited. Natasha and I talked about makeup and clothes while we waited. Natasha told me she wore either "Mary Kay" or "Avon" make-up. This was surprising and funny to me. I didn't realize that Mary Kay and Avon were "universal."

We found out that Yanna was in training to become an interpreter and that was why she was there. She asked us if we minded her "tagging along," which of course we didn't. Still waiting for the Department of Ministry and Education to open, we walked around outside while Natasha pointed out landmarks and gave us some history about the architecture and the buildings. We were on the main street of Zaporizhia. Natasha explained that during World War II, much of Zaporizhia had been bombed and they were still rebuilding. This main street was one of the few streets that they had been able to either refurbish or rebuild. They took great pride in it. It was the only really modern looking street we saw, and very clean. Once again though, if you looked around the corner or went over a block or two it was total poverty and filth!

At 11:00 we went back to the Department of Ministry and Education to meet with the director. Luba instructed us to be very quiet and polite, speak only when spoken to, and answer questions very respectfully. Everyone there looked so serious and downright crabby or mad.

NO ONE smiled and we felt like we were being "glared" at. Natasha and Yanna, seeing how nervous we were, kept winking at us and making jokes. Discreetly they would make fun of the crabby ladies, imitating their scowling faces and telling us not to worry. This helped us relax and laugh a bit.

A little boy about eight years old was in the small waiting room with us. He kept smiling at us. It made me miss my boys. He was holding a piece of candy in his hand and he tried to give it to me. I told him "no thank you; you keep it," but he insisted on me having it. I popped the candy in my mouth, and smiling back I thanked him. Our eyes seemed to lock for the longest time. I could see the loneliness in his eyes and his desperate need to connect with someone. We could not communicate in words, but our feelings were communicated through our eyes. It was very emotional for me. This would not be the last child this would happen with in the Ukraine. Many more would come. Children have that wonderful openness to them. They have not "hardened" yet. They have not become bitter like the women in this government office.

After hours of waiting, we finally received clearance. We would now go to another government office to have the papers looked over, cleared, and notarized, now by the Department of Ministries' lawyer. We had to pay for all of these services also. We signed more and more papers. Luba was upset that everything was taking so long. This was when we first realized how fortunate we were to have Luba working for us.

Luba is a very "take charge," aggressive woman. Everywhere we go she seems to be fighting a difficult, complex battle to clear the way for us. Natasha is very annoyed by Luba and calls her "pushy and rude". In the end though we would be very grateful for Luba's pushiness"

At the lawyer's office we found out about a problem with our marriage license. Apparently the notarized copy of our official marriage license, the one I had gone out of my way to get from our local courthouse, had somehow not made it into our file to the Ukraine. Gregg and I sat frozen while Luba and the Ukrainian attorney argued about this. I thought I was going to throw up while we waited to see if the lawyer was going to accept the "souvenir" copy of our marriage license. Thank God, she decided to accept it!

Finally at about 3:00 in the afternoon we were ready to go to the orphanage. Back we all piled into the teeny, tiny cab! We wound through what seemed like miles of filth, falling down flats and buildings. We were struck by all the people and especially the children (very young children) roaming the streets. Garbage was everywhere. There were open markets throughout every neighborhood. Old ladies selling flowers, vegetables, embroidered linens, books, clothing, and more. The people on the buses looked sad, angry, and very tired. I asked Natasha why hardly anyone in the Ukraine smiles. She said, "Because they have a lot of problems. We work hard and still do not have enough money for our rent and food."

Natasha pointed to the dirty, barely standing flats. In order to afford to live in one of those, everyone in the family must work, she told us. It is common for grandparents, cousins, aunts, and uncles to all live together in a one, or two bedroom flat; it is the only way they can afford it. I am looking at these flats people call "home" and am thinking I wouldn't want to spend one night there, let alone raise a family there. I would compare them to the ghettos in New York city.

"I hate it," said Natasha, "My husband and I are saving to move into a nicer flat in a better area."

Natasha and her husband are both college graduates with good jobs but they barely get by. Yanna, who is also a college graduate and teaches school at a university, said she lived with her father and could never afford to move out on her own. They both added that women in the Ukraine, even if they have the same jobs as men, are paid substantially less. They knew of no women who lived alone, let alone own a car or any of the things women in America take for granted.

We finally pulled into the orphanage. My heart was pounding and I felt light-headed. Gregg and I squeezed each other's hand. The orphanage had a tall fence around it. There was children's artwork painted on the large, dirty, old cement building, making it look a little more cheerful. The name of the orphanage is Coheyko, which means "sunny." It looked more like a very old hospital than an orphanage to me. I couldn't believe it was "home" to over three hundred children.

When we got out of the cab, Luba told us to wait outside while she went in and made sure the director was ready for us. I looked around and realized that I had not seen any signs of children yet. There was a dog in a fenced area that barked at us. Gregg and I agreed that he was definitely a good watchdog as he was the biggest, scariest dog we had ever seen!

As we walked around the grounds we saw playground equipment on one side of the building. There was some grass and picnic tables in one area. As we walked by one "wing" of the building I heard babies crying. I was trying not to cry at this point and was feeling emotional and scared.

Luba came out and said the director was ready to meet with us. We would have to go over Olga's records and sign some papers before we could meet her. We are only allowed to walk through certain areas of the orphanage; we were never allowed to go in any rooms where the children were.

We went with Luba, Natasha, and Yanna into the director's office. She was a middle-aged, blond, attractive, and friendly lady. Everyone that worked in the orphanage had a lab coat on; it looked very "sterile" and again I felt like we were in a World War II movie.

We all sat down and the director explained (through our interpreters) that we would go through Olga's chart together. It was important that we understand all of Olga's history. The director said that after giving birth to Olga, Olga's mother walked out of the "birthing center" three days later. She had not given accurate information to the birthing center regarding her real name, address, etc. It had all proven to be false information. The birthing center, along with the Ukrainian government, were never able to locate Olga's mother or any family members. The name the mother listed on the form as her own was exactly the same name she gave her baby, Kryla Olga Seragina.

The Ukrainian government does not release any of its children for international adoption until they are at least a year old. The Ukraine, as with most countries, tries very hard to keep their children in their own country. They try for the first year of an orphaned baby's life to place them with a family in the Ukraine. This does not happen very often because there are very few couples or families who can afford to adopt in the Ukraine.

At this point in our meeting with the director we were feeling very happy, excited, and anxious to me Olga. Then the director began talking about Olga's medical conditions. It was difficult trying to understand everything the director was saying because it was going from her to our interpreters to us. Natasha and Yanna were nervous about interpreting the medical lingo because they wanted to make sure they were understanding and thus providing us with accurate information.

We were told of several conditions and diagnoses. Olga would "most likely" have permanent damage to her central nervous system, which was the consequence of toxic hypoxia. Basically poor prenatal care prevented sufficient oxygen and nutrients from reaching the baby during pregnancy. Olga had rickets and anemia (most likely due to poor nutrition), and pyelonephritis (inflammation of the kidneys, most likely due to dehydration). At this point Gregg and I had turned pale and were barely breathing. We were told we would be meeting a "beautiful, perfectly healthy baby girl," so we were not prepared for any of this.

I have a background in the medical field so I was processing this information a little better than Gregg. From what I knew, the only diagnosis I was really concerned about was the permanent damage to the central nervous system. I kept telling Gregg to calm down, we would have to wait and see. The director said we should expect our little girl to be "a bit delayed." At one point Natasha used the word "retarded," which again alarmed us. Natasha told us later that the English dictionary she was using to interpret showed "delayed" and "retarded" as words that could be "interchangeable." We later told her they were much different to us.

I honestly thought at one point I was either going to start crying, throw up, pass out, or all three. I think Gregg felt the same way. We were trying so hard to stay positive and process all this information. When the director was through she asked Natasha why we looked so "serious" and "upset"? Natasha said we were worried about these diagnoses. The director patted my leg and told Natasha to tell me to relax, that Olga was beautiful and, as a matter of fact, she looked just like me.

We were exhausted and extremely apprehensive at this point, but we told them we were ready to meet our girl now. Gregg and I took deep breaths and we headed down the long, dark hallway to meet Olga. Again our hearts were pounding. There are hardly words to describe the mix of emotions we were feeling.

As I mentioned before, the orphanage was divided into separate area's for different age group's of children. The doors were all locked so no one could get to the children without the proper clearance. It seemed more like a prison than an orphanage. We knocked on the door to the area where the "toddlers" were, ages one to two years old. We were admitted to a dressing room area but could see through one of the doors to a fairly large room with a huge wooden playpen with toddlers playing in and around it. We were asked to take off our shoes and told we could step inside but not to approach the children. We would be allowed to watch them play for a short time. With tears in my eyes I watched those precious little ones playing, wondering which one was our little girl.

The only picture we'd seen of Olga at that point was one that was over a year old. Swaddled in her blanket, you could barely see her face. Olga was now fourteen months old. One of the caregivers called her name. It sounded like "Olya" in English. The Ukrainians say their "g's" like we pronounce our "y's." Very suspiciously Olga looked our way. I will never forget the way she looked at us. She did not trust us one single bit and did not want anything to do with us.

While many of the other toddlers came running right up to us with their arms stretched out to be held, Olga took off to the far side of the room, "glaring" at us. She seemed very scared and suspicious of us. Gregg said to me, "Oh honey, she is a beautiful little girl," and I agreed! I could hardly speak as I was so emotional. I don't know who was more frightened, me or Olga. The caregiver went and picked Olga up and brought her to us. Olga clung to her, still wanting absolutely nothing to do with us. The caregiver said, "Look, Olga, this is your mamma!" I remember thinking how much I did not deserve that title as of yet.

The title "mamma" is something I think many women might take for granted. It's a term many children take for granted also. I don't think I will ever quit melting when Olga calls me Mamma. The caregiver told us (through our interpreters) that she would go and get Olga ready and we could take her outside for a little while and get to know her.

We stepped back out into the waiting room to wait for them to dress her to go outside. Natasha, Luba, and Yanna were very excited for us. "She is beautiful," they all said. "She does look like you." I was still too overwhelmed to talk much. When they brought Olga out, she was bundled up tightly. She had on three layers of clothes and a tight scarf on her head. She knew something was going on and she was not OK with any of it. She was frowning and her lips were tightly pursed. She did not want to come to me and started to cry.

I realized I needed to just take her and go. I held her tightly and we dashed out the door. We wandered back down the long dark hallways, not really sure where to go. We headed outside as it was a very nice day. Luba seemed to switch from the role of attorney to "expert in child care." She started telling us to "keep her head covered," "hold her this way," "talk to her this way," "you need to do this," "you need to do that." Suddenly I was annoyed with Luba and wanted her to go away and let me get to know my daughter. I wanted to tell her, "This is my daughter. I know what to do. I raised two boys, so please back off!"

Finally Gregg and I got some time and space alone with Olga. We wandered off to a grassy area where there were a few trees and flowers. Olga was scared. She clung tightly to me and trembled. She studied us carefully. Tears ran down her cheeks. She was starting to be "OK" with me but was really scared of Gregg. Her eyes were saying, "Why should I trust you guys? Who are you anyway?"

It was very warm outside, so I tried to take the tight handkerchief off her head so we could get a better look at her. Luba appeared out of nowhere to reprimand us for taking her hat off. After our scolding we put the kerchief back on. Olga was acting as if she had never been outside before. She looked around scared and curious. I was showing Olga the birdies, the leaves, and the grass! Gregg picked her a flower and tried to hand it to her. She was very skeptical but she took it from him. Gregg snapped a picture of her with her eyes still suspicious and tearful. She held the flower and we saw the first hint of a smile.

Our first meeting with Ola, our very sad and untrusting
little girl

I watched her carefully and her reactions to noises. I watched her eyes and studied her dexterity as she reached for things. She seemed alert, coordinated, and healthy. She picked up leaves easily and studied them carefully. When she did smile her nose wrinkled up and her front teeth looked kind of big. My first thought was she looked like a squirrel when she smiled. (An adorable squirrel, I might add!)

My fears about the diagnoses we heard about in the director's office were starting to ease a little. We still had so many questions though. We wanted to savor the moment but we were still scared. Our time with Olga went by quickly and Luba came to tell us we needed to take her back in. Olga and I were still studying each other intently. We held each other tightly and looked deep into each other's eyes.

When I went to hand her back to the caregiver, Olga clung to me for just a moment, almost not wanting to let go. The caregiver thought that was a very good sign and acted surprised. We waved good-bye as Olga studied us closely, watching us go. Gregg and I were emotionally exhausted. When we got outside, Luba kicked back into her "attorney mode" and told us she'd like to try to get the papers filed today before 5:00 so the adoption procedure could begin immediately!

Gregg and I were overwhelmed with questions. We were still worried about some of the diagnoses we had heard earlier. Luba explained that we could start the legal work and get things "rolling" while we continued to work through any questions and concerns. The adoption could be stopped at any time before the final decision with the judge was made. It would be good to at least get things started, she said.

Absolutely exhausted mentally and physically, Gregg and I agreed to take Luba's advice and try to file the paperwork before 5:00. It was 4:00 in the afternoon in Zaporizhia, but it was actually 2:00 in the morning to us. We headed off in a daze to make it to yet another attorney's office to file our petition to adopt Olga. The next hour at the government office was a blur for us. We tried to push our concerns aside and muddle through the paperwork. Deep down, for some reason, we believed it would all work out.

Natasha told us the next day that we were very hard to communicate with that last hour at the attorney's office. She said we asked the same questions over and over and had "blank stares" on our faces. We had to laugh at this. Gregg was absolutely incoherent! I've never seen him like that! At one point I took him aside and shook him. "I need you to pull yourself together," I told him. "We need to get through this last attorney today and we can go back to the hotel and collapse." When we finally got back to our hotel, we decided we needed to have some dinner before heading for bed. I told Gregg to order me something, I didn't care what! I could not make one more decision today. As usual we didn't get what we thought we ordered but my stomach was so tied up in knots I couldn't eat anyway. Gregg and I wanted so much to talk about the amazing events of the day, but we agreed we were too exhausted to discuss our concerns. We agreed we just needed a good night's sleep. When we got back to our room I called room service and asked the waitress if she could bring me some hot chocolate and toast. (Something that would be soothing and help me go to sleep). A while later she brought me a melted chocolate bar and some dried bread! I guess that is hot chocolate and toast in the Ukraine. I took a sleeping pill and fell into bed. We did manage to get a good night's sleep. Oh my goodness, I believe in the saying, "what a difference a day makes!" Gregg and I awoke ready to take on our adoption "project" again. We were rejuvenated and anxious to get back to the orphanage and visit Olga. We felt so much better about everything and our positive attitudes returned.

We spoke with Natasha and asked if she could work with Luba in making arrangements to have a doctor come to the orphanage and examine Olga. We had been told ahead of time, buy our agency, that this would be totally acceptable. A doctor separate from the orphanage was encouraged. Natasha said she had a pediatrician she loved and trusted and that she would contact her for us. Gregg and I went to breakfast and waited for Natasha and Luba to call us back and let us know our schedule for the day.

I called my friends at our medical clinic back home to get their opinion on the diagnoses we were given on Olga. The nurses there are good friends and agreed to talk to the doctors (whom are also good friends), and that we should call back later. I was so grateful to have their help. Natasha told us that the pediatrician she recommended was happy to meet us at the orphanage and examine Olga that evening. Gregg and I were amazed by this. In the United States getting a pediatrician to meet you anywhere outside of their office would be quite a task. You would most likely need appointments, referrals, insurance pre-authorizations, etc., and it would take all kinds of time and money.

We met in the lobby and again all five of us piled into the tiny cab and made our way to the orphanage. We couldn't wait to see Olga again. We hoped we would be better able to interact with her now that we were rested, more relaxed, and coherent. As we walked in she was playing with the other children. Again, she spotted us and immediately gave us that same suspicious, almost ticked off look! It was like she was thinking, "It's those people again. Why are they looking at ME that way?" Walking to the far corner of the room like she had done before, she glared at us. It was a sunny, nice day, we had shorts and tee shirts on, but again they bundled her up in at least four layers of clothing and a stocking hat. I looked at Gregg and said, "Do they think we're taking her snowmobiling?" She could hardly move.

She reluctantly came to me but was shaking and started to cry. Again I held her tight and we headed outside. We tried to find a quiet place that we could be alone with Olga and try to get to know her. We found an area of grass by an old, crumbled down concrete building and sat down on the ground. Olga was holding on to me so tightly I couldn't pry her loose enough to even see her face! It was hard to try to talk to her or interact in any way. I just held her tight and listened to her little heart pounding with fear. I tried my best to comfort and calm her. She finally let me sit her on my lap so Gregg and I could talk to her. She "sort of" trusted me, but was still scared to death of Gregg. She continued to give him quite the glare!

Over the next hour she relaxed a little and we managed to get a few small smiles between glares. When Gregg tried to take her she screamed hysterically, but he took her and walked around until she calmed down. Her eyes were still saying, "Why should I trust YOU?" After spending a few hours with Olga, Gregg and I both agreed that she seemed to be a perfectly healthy baby. Her eyes were clear and bright, she responded to every noise, she looked around acutely aware of everything and everyone. She reached for branches and picked up rocks. We talked to all the birdies, and a few butterflies. Our fears were subsiding. It was hard to take her back inside.

As I gave her back to the caregiver Olga looked back at me a little confused and I think she didn't want me to leave. She gave me a very small smile. She was very anxious to get back to her friends though. As we were leaving that morning Gregg and I were feeling much better about Olga. Natasha confirmed that we would meet with her pediatrician back at the orphanage that evening. We were anxious for her to be examined and have our beliefs confirmed that she was just fine. We wanted so much to believe we would be able to take her home, feed her a little better, and with enough love she would be a healthy, happy little girl. Even before she saw the doctor, somehow Gregg and I knew everything was going to be OK.

We went and had lunch and came back to spend the afternoon with Olga. At each visit she got a little more relaxed with us and us with her. Gregg and I became more and more positive that this was the baby girl we were supposed to find and love forever!

Natasha's pediatrician met us at the orphanage that evening. First she read through Olga's chart. She did not seem that concerned about anything she read. She said all of Olga's diagnoses were very common and what you would expect to see of any child in an orphanage. She had the nurses undress Olga and she spent the next half-hour examining her as we watched. When she was finished, the nurse took Olga, who was now very mad about all the poking and prodding that had taken place, and got her dressed, while we talked to the doctor.

The doctor looked at us and said confidently, "I do not see any signs of anything you should be worried about. The only thing this baby needs is love. She will be just fine." We were more than ready to give this child all the love she would need. Apparently the doctors in the Ukraine use the same "common diagnoses" for many of the children they examine in the orphanages. After visiting with the doctor, we came to understand that the doctors in the Ukraine communicate differently than what you might see in the U.S. today. They often "speculate," which made sense to me, because they had referred to Olga's birth mother's "poor prenatal care"; yet they knew nothing about her prenatal care for sure, as there were no records. Obviously, that was more of an assumption, based on what they normally see in birthing centers and with orphans.

Basically, they try to "cover all possibilities," especially for adoption purposes. They tend to lean toward the "worst case scenarios" with their diagnoses. We still could not be totally sure about Olga's medical condition, but somehow, we just weren't that worried anymore. We made the final commitment at that moment to accept Olga as our daughter, come what may! We would deal with whatever we needed to, but this was our girl now!

As we left the orphanage we felt very positive. Luba arranged for us to have our first meeting with the judge the next day in the afternoon. This would just be a preliminary hearing but we were very nervous. I asked Natasha if she knew of any other hotels that might be a little closer to the orphanage, maybe a little bit nicer too. It was costing us a lot of time and money going back and forth to the orphanage three times a day. She said her husband made a lot of arrangement for clients when they traveled, and she would talk to him and let us know.

We went back to the hotel to freshen up and to call the clinic and talk to our family doctor about the diagnoses we had given them the day before on Olga. It was fun to talk to someone back home at the clinic where I had worked. The nurse had talked to our family doctor for us. They all agreed that the diagnoses were most likely nothing to worry about and that we should be able to deal with anything we needed to when we got home. They were very reassuring and made us feel even better about things. They explained each diagnosis in a way that helped me to understand it better.

I was so grateful for their input. The doctors and nurses told us they didn't think they had ever done a "consult" so far away, and never in the Ukraine! They, of course, did not charge us for their time and wished us good luck. I told them we would be in for a visit as soon as we got home. Their caring and kindness was felt strongly even though we were many, many miles apart.

Gregg and I decided to go and have some dinner that night at a little pizza parlor we had passed a couple of times. I was imagining and craving the kind of pizza you would expect to have back home. As usual, this pizza tasted totally different. Everything tasted totally different in the Ukraine. It is hard to explain exactly what tasted so different. They use different cheeses and spices and everything is very greasy. We noticed a lot people staring at us. This is how "foreigners" must feel when they visit our country. It is natural to stare at people when they are speaking a different language. It is just curiosity. As Gregg and I were finishing our pizza, we noticed two very beautiful young women walk in and be seated. As I said before, the women in the Ukraine are beautiful and dress "very sexy!" Gregg especially noticed them all. The two women sat down and began to visit back and forth and looked like good friends. A few minutes later they began screaming at each other, which of course got our attention. At this point one of the women got up and began breaking these heavy, thick plates over the top of the other woman's head! The screaming worsened and plates and pieces of plates were now being thrown and broken over each other's heads, along with kicking, punching, biting, and much cursing between the two of them.

Gregg and I sat stunned. The waitress called the police, who arrived very quickly and heavily armed. Both women were arrested and carted off in police cars. Gregg and I felt like we were the only ones in the restaurant who seemed "alarmed" by what happened. Most of the other diners seemed to watch without much expression and go back to eating like nothing had happened. So this was an exciting dinner for us. Wide-eyed and frightened we returned to our hotel. After we got back in our room we were able to laugh about the bizarre event we had just witnessed.

8

"The legal Process"

The next day we were up bright and early again. We had breakfast and were ready to visit our Olga. Every day we were amazed at how much more Olga was relaxing around us; we were really starting to get to know her. Her sweetness and fun personality were coming through. We also came to realize that this little girl was very, very smart. It was becoming obvious to us that our Olga was a very sharp little girl. (No we are not prejudiced!) She watched everyone and everything with great curiosity. She was always a little guarded and you could see the sense of "survival" in her eyes. Gregg and I were amazed at the way they fed the children. They were all put in the large, sturdy playpen in the middle of the room. One of the caregivers had a big bowl of "mush" and another had a big bowl of apple juice. They went around the playpen with one big spoon in each bowl and fed the children. Around the play pen they went with the toddlers looking like little "baby birds", their mouths open waiting for their spoonful to make its way around to them.

Olga was not aggressive with the other children at all. As we watched her play with the other children we could see that if you were playing with a toy and another child wanted that toy, you were better off handing it over or you could end up with the toy being bashed over your head!! Our little Olga had probably learned the hard way, early on, that no toy was worth getting hit for. Olga always gave the toy up pretty quickly without resistance. Olga would later learn to "hold her own" after we got home and she can now "fight for toys" with the best of them.

After a great day with Olga we talked to Natasha about having dinner with her and her husband "Ruslan." Natasha had spoken to Ruslan about dinner and finding us a hotel a little closer to the orphanage. They asked if we would like to meet at a lovely bed and breakfast that had a very nice restaurant. It was one of Natasha's and Ruslan's favorite places. Ruslan had made arrangements for a lot of his clients to stay there. He said it was on a river and very peaceful. We could have dinner and look at the rooms. If we liked it he would make arrangements for us to move there. With all the emotional issues we were going through moving to a nice, quiet bed and breakfast on the water sounded wonderful. We were looking forward to a night out with Natasha and meeting her husband, Ruslan.

The taxi picked us up that evening and again we had a wild ride to meet Natasha and Ruslan. We jolted across highways, down dirt roads (more like "trails"), bounced through potholes, dodged buses, (not to mention people), and finally arrived at the bed and breakfast. We knew we would never get used to the way they drive there. When we pulled into the bed and breakfast called "Puua" we immediately loved it. It was on a river and the bed and breakfast sat within a small inlet right on the water.

It was decorated very cute with grass hut style roofing and a water fountain out front. There was a main building and cottages surrounding it. There were old wagons and picnic tables, an indoor restaurant area, and a lovely outdoor seating area on the water. It was very quaint and reminiscent of old Russia. Of course they had the loud disco music playing all the time, which took away from the quaint, quiet, peacefulness of the place for us. Ruslan told us later that all restaurants have live music, always. If it did not have music it was not considered a decent place.

We decided to dine outside, as it was a nice evening. Natasha looked beautiful as usual and we instantly loved Ruslan. Ruslan was an agricultural chemical dealer, which seemed very coincidental to me. Immediately Gregg and Ruslan went straight to "farming." Ruslan sold a variety of things, one being "Round-up." He was a dealer for Monsanto products, many of which Gregg uses. So the guys talked "agriculture" while Natasha tried to show me how to put on lip liner properly.

Natasha was obsessed with helping me become more "feminine." Ruslan asked if he could order us his favorite appetizer and we told him "that would be great as we were starving." He ordered it from the waitress in Ukrainian, along with our drinks. Gregg had become quite fond of Russian style beer and I was now hooked on the vodka tonics (the Vodka is very smooth there). When the appetizer came it looked quite yummy. It was some type of meat sliced, cooked and served with a creamy dill sauce. Dill is very popular there and everything is covered with it.

As I nibbled on the appetizer I politely asked what it was exactly. "Pickled cow tongue," our friends answered, smiling proudly. Trying to not spit it across the table or show my repulsion, I smiled back and said, "Oh, It's very good." Gregg was not bothered by the fact it was cow tongue, but Ruslan and Natasha could see that I was less than thrilled.

This was one of many times that I saw how proud the Ukrainians are of everything in their country including their food. I tried to keep nibbling on the pickled tongue so that I wouldn't offend them, but I couldn't eat it.

We enjoyed getting to know Natasha and Ruslan. We were amazed at how easily we visited with them and how much we had in common. Natasha and I became the best of friends. Later, Natasha and Yanna told me that they did not think they liked Americans until they met us. We had a wonderful evening with our new friends (except for the millions of mosquitoes that joined us!)

We moved the next day to this charming bed and breakfast. It was much more relaxing, comfortable, and closer to the orphanage. It was calming to wake up and look out at the water. It looked like many of their employees lived behind the main building in a little travel trailer.

We noticed that many of the workers in the Ukraine had to work very long shifts. The waitresses and waiters were young, and it looked like they stayed there and maybe worked one week on, one week off. Perhaps it was more cost effective not to have to drive back and forth, but the same people waited on us morning, noon and night. By the end of the week, they looked very tired.

There were men building a cement patio off of the restaurant. They were breaking up the rocks and mixing the cement themselves. The same men were out there working from the minute the sun was up until dark. One of the men working was quite elderly, yet worked just as long and hard as his younger coworkers. Here again is an example of how much we take for granted.

The Ukraine has only been its own country for a little more than a decade, separate, that is from the Soviet Union. They are still working on setting up all their government programs similar to what we have like welfare, Medicare, and Social Security. Everyone works very hard in the Ukraine and many of them will have to work this hard until the day they die. They have no money to retire. This, to me, is the saddest and hardest part of our visit to the Ukraine, seeing so many of the elderly and the children struggle to survive. I watched a very old man one afternoon, crawl underneath a car to retrieve a dirty, squished strawberry with gravel in it to eat. He had probably worked hard all his life and did not deserve to be so desolate, poor and hungry. They are so behind in technology that everything is still basically done by hand, the "old fashioned way." I don't think we realize all the specialty tools we have available to us, that make our lives so much easier here.

Staying at the bed and breakfast, we became familiar with the Ukraine's "wildlife." We were in a whole new world here on the water's edge. We saw huge cats and heard wild dogs everywhere. We had read before we went to the Ukraine that they had packs of wild dogs running everywhere and to be very careful to avoid them. We never saw them but could hear them everywhere, in the country and the middle of the city. The frogs by the bay were huge and they literally barked rather than croak like what I was used to.

We spent the next three days in Zaporizhia going back and forth to the orphanage, working on wrapping up all the legal paperwork, and trying to enjoy the country and its diverse culture. Between our visits with Olga, Natasha and I would visit. Yanna had lost her passport so she was unable to work with us anymore. In the Ukraine you must have your passport with you at all times. If you lose it you are unable to work or do anything. Even if you were born and raised there, you still must have your passport on you at all times.

Yanna felt so bad! We didn't get to see her very much after that. She showed up and tagged along once in a while, but she was not legally supposed to be working with us at all. There is a huge fine also when you lose your passport and have to request a new one. She was so upset and we felt really bad for her.

Yanna and I talked a lot about her life there. She lived with her dad, whom she adored. She said she loved taking care of him. She was frustrated with her boyfriend because he drank too much.

This was a common problem for many of the young men we saw in the Ukraine. It became clear that the problem with alcohol, poverty and the lack of education played heavily into the reason there were so many orphans. They all go hand in hand. There are kegs of beer sold on every street corner and there seemed to be no age limit. Yanna said birth control was not discussed much with young people. There are also strip clubs on every street corner, which reflects the "moral structural" problems in the country. Gregg made the mistake to "teasingly" suggest one night that we check out one of the strip clubs. He knew immediately by the look on my face that this was not a funny, let alone a good, suggestion.

"We are here in this country to adopt an orphaned child, which is a direct consequence of what you are now saying we should go and support and spend our money on?" (I said this in a hissing tone with daggers coming from my eyes.) "Of course not," he replied. "I was just kidding." (That's his story and he's sticking to it"!)

One afternoon, between our afternoon and evening visits to the orphanage, Gregg and Luba visited some government offices and completed yet more paperwork. I did not need to sign these papers, so Natasha and Yanna decided they would take me shopping. We first walked through the open market, which I had grown to hate. I felt sorry for the people, especially all the old ladies sitting in the heat, on the ground every day selling flowers and vegetables from their gardens. The booths there sold mostly used and very worn clothing so that did not excite me much.

The worst part of the open markets for me was the meat market section. Skinned chickens, pork, and sausages hung from the eaves outside for sale. Flies were all over them and they smelled awful. Another thing we take for granted here is refrigeration. Refrigeration is too expensive and is scarce in the Ukraine. Most of their meats are eventually smoked to make them last longer.

Natasha suggested we go to the mall. As I mentioned before everyone had told us to dress very plain and not flashy so as not to draw attention to ourselves, so I had packed dark clothing and flat dark shoes. Natasha and Yanna hated my black, flat Keds tennis shoes. Natasha pronounced my name in a funny, almost southern like drawl. She'd say "Sheraall," "Why you dress like a boy?"

Compared to the way that Natasha dressed and most of the other Ukrainian women, I did in fact dress like a boy. Natasha always looked beautiful; she dressed like all the women there, very feminine, usually her flat belly and belly button ring showing. Her long dark hair and makeup were always perfect. She told me she really "NEEDED" to take me shopping.

As I said before, there is either the very expensive designer clothing at the malls or the used clothing in the open markets, not much in between. So Natasha and Yanna took me to the mall. The malls are filled with outrageously expensive designer clothes, shoes, and house wares. They do not like you to touch anything. The clerks ask you to point to whatever you want to see, and then they hold it up for you. Most of the shoppers do not try things on either.

Yanna and Natasha showed me all the leather pointy-toed, high-heeled shoes and tried to get me to try them on, (which I did just for fun). They didn't understand that stilettos are just "not me." I ended up buying some nice, flat black sandals that they thought were ugly. They showed me all kinds of shoes and clothing they loved but that I thought looked like something a hooker would wear.

They shook their heads and teased me about my boring taste in clothing. I told them that actually my sisters and friends back home think I am kind of "prissy." I told them that one of my sisters tells me constantly I am way too much of a "girly girl." They laughed and shook their heads in disbelief.

I did manage to find a mid-length black cotton blend dress with subtle water-colored flowers on it that happened to be on sale. They were not thrilled with that purchase either, but I was happy with it and thought it would be a good outfit to wear when we went to court to finalize our adoption. Natasha and Yanna were so disappointed in me. They had not managed to get me into a sexy, Ukrainian outfit and they felt like failures!

Natasha and I spent almost every moment together except when Gregg and I were at the orphanage with Olga. Natasha shared with me the heartbreaking story of how she and her husband had lost their beautiful son to brain cancer when he was only ten years old. Tears flowed freely down both of our cheeks as she told me how hard it was to care for him and eventually lose him to this horrible disease.

Ruslan was going to school and working in another country when their son became ill and he could not miss work or they would lose their much-needed health insurance. Natasha was all alone most of the time and carried the huge burden of getting their son to doctors and hospitals by herself. He eventually was in a wheelchair, which made it even more difficult for her to take care of him alone.

She told me about one of the lowest moments for her, when the elevator in their building was out of order and they lived on the sixth floor. She had to carry her son, his wheelchair, and any groceries or other essentials up and down the stairs to the sixth floor. It was "hell," she said. At this point Natasha looked at me, both of us sobbing and flexed the muscles in her arms. "I was really BUFF though", she said proudly!! I smiled, laughing a little and hugged her.

She showed me pictures and shared with me how she taught her son to swim when he was only three. Natasha and I held hands and hugged a lot as she shared story after story about her son dying. In the end, she told me, while in the hospital her son began asking about heaven. She said she didn't know what to tell him at first, but that the words somehow just came to her. She told him it was "very beautiful in heaven" and that "he would be very happy there and not have any more pain." She said, "Our virgin Mary will take care of you until I can join you there someday."

She said her son seemed to take great comfort in her words. Right before her son slipped into a coma and died, he told Natasha that he was ready to go to this place called heaven. She said he was very peaceful when he passed on and that she was grateful for that.

Natasha said it was very hard for Ruslan, because when he left his son was very healthy and strong and when he came back, he did not even look like the same boy. His son was now very frail, dying, and only able to sit in a wheelchair or lie in a bed. They did everything they could for their son but they could not save him.

Natasha said she had a complete nervous breakdown after that. She drank heavily everyday. She barely got through the days. Ruslan was very worried about her. Finally one night she said she had a vision. She said she had fallen asleep and that maybe it was just a dream, but that it was amazingly real and vivid. She said she saw her son sitting on Mary's lap. They were surrounded by other happy, laughing children. She said her son looked so happy and healthy. When she awoke she said she had a strong, overwhelming sense of peace. From that moment on she was better able to cope.

She told me that it was very hard for her to believe in God now. She could not understand how he could be so cruel. She told me that doing things to help other people, like helping us adopt Olga, helped her heal and believe again. I told her how much I loved and admired her strength. I told her there was just no way to convey how grateful I was for her help and how privileged I felt to know her. Natasha and I agreed we felt like we were "sisters" and we would remain so always and forever in our hearts. She told me she had always wanted a sister, and now she had one. I will never be able to put into words the love and connection I felt with Natasha. I think of her often. My beautiful and amazing new sister Natasha.

Natasha arranged to take us to the museum in Zaporizhia one day while we were there. It was the only day we did not visit the orphanage until evening. It proved to be a much needed relaxing, very interesting, and educational day. The museum was absolutely fascinating. We saw artifacts dating back thousands of years, religious items dating back before Christ.

Most Ukrainians are strong Christians. The "soldiers" or "warriors" there—the people who fought to "free" the Ukraine—are referred to as "Cossacks." As they still are today, they were very proud, hard-working people.

During World War II, much of the Ukraine was destroyed by air raids. The country had to work very hard to restore their monuments and historical buildings. They are very proud of their dam on the river Dneproges. Natasha kept calling it their "dump" and we had to explain to her that there is a big difference between a dam and a dump in America! She thanked us for helping her with her English.

The dam was built by hand without the help of modern technology. They mixed the cement by "hand" and by "foot." People took turns mixing the cement with their feet. The women made up "dances" to help with this difficult task. They would take turns dancing to music and entertaining the workers as they mixed the cement with their feet. The dam now supports the largest hydro power plant in the Ukraine.

The Ukrainian people are very artistic. The artwork, including paintings, embroiders, and pottery, were gorgeous. Gregg and I walked through the museum absolutely fascinated. Natasha did a great job narrating our tour and we learned much about the Ukraine, its history, and its people. It was fun to get a better idea of Olga's ancestors and their history. We can share it with her when she is older.

We laughed at how all the Cossacks had high foreheads and receding hairlines. The Cossacks wore their hair straight up, making them look like something out of a horror film! When our daughter is mad now we call her "our little Cossack."

We all went to lunch to have what Natasha said was going to be "authentic" Ukrainian food. The restaurant was decorated with carved wooden Cossack statues, swords, Ukrainian musical instruments, and wild boars everywhere. The waiters and waitresses were dressed in old-fashioned Ukrainian costumes and were so friendly. Many of the wines made in the Ukraine are very good, especially the reds.

We had a Ukrainian-style "soup" or "stew" made with pork and tomatoes and lots of veggies. It came with yummy homemade rolls. As I mentioned, everything is "greasy" there, so there was a layer of "oil" floating on top of the stew. We were starting to get used to that, so we stirred it up and gobbled it down. It was delicious. We thanked Natasha for the wonderful day and told her how much it meant to us. It was one of the most relaxing, enjoyable days we had in the Ukraine and gave us a better and more positive view of the country and its people.

We had somewhat of a routine now. We visited the orphanage from 9:00 to 11:00 in the mornings, also from 2:00 to 4:00 in the afternoons, and from 6:00 to 7:00 in the evenings. We also got to know the other parents who were in the process of adopting. They were people from all around the world. It was fun for all of us to watch as our children started to bond with us.

Most of the other couples spoke little or no English but we communicated well despite this. During the day when the weather was nice we would take our children outside to play, and we walked around and got to know each other. When we would arrive at the orphanage, the nurses would sing out, "Olya, Mommy and Daddy are here!" Eventually she began to warm up to us and would come to us ready to play. It was such a relief after those early visits when she was so frightened and uncomfortable with us. We watched as her cute little personality started to emerge and we got to know her better. We could see what a sweet, funny little girl we had.

One night at the orphanage we all gathered in the large meeting room to play with our kids. We happily sat around on the dirty floor together. It was a very dark, stormy night. Some of the couples brought toys like rattles, balls and "blowing bubbles" to share. We learned early on to bring enough for all of the kids because if you only brought a toy for your child the rest of the children were devastated and would fight over the toy! It was fun to watch the toddlers chase the "bubbles" around.

We were not supposed to bring any kind of food into the orphanage, but many of us snuck thinks in, like cookies. Gregg had learned that the way to Olga's heart was with bananas. She loved bananas. At first the only way Olga would have anything to do with Gregg was if he had a banana. She was starting to be less and less afraid of Gregg and finally would let him hold her once in a while.

Gregg and I have never in our lives seen rain pour down like it did that night. It has never rained here like it did there that night. In less than an hour, we saw it rain more that it ever has in a month on our farm in eastern Oregon! Talk about a "downpour." There were huge bolts of lightning that lit up the whole sky, and thunder so loud and powerful it shook the building. When we left later that night we walked through water over our ankles. Water and garbage flooded down the streets. It was disgusting having to wade through it to find a taxi!

It was cozy and warm inside the orphanage that night though. We all cuddled with our new little ones as we watched the storm. It was always so much fun to watch everyone playing with their kids and witness the bonds becoming stronger for each family with their new sons and daughters. Each of us was smiling and happy for one another, sharing the love and laughter.

It was cold and dark outside, but warm inside this room full of new families. We felt a strong connection with these people that we hardly knew and could barely communicate with. We communicated directly from the heart through our eyes and with warm, encouraging smiles. We took pictures for each other. We would clap with joy when our children ran to us for the first time. We would laugh and cry as we witnessed, first hugs and first kisses. We tied each other's children's shoe laces, picked up and comforted the ones who fell down, worked out "confrontations" over toys, and handed out a lot of Kleenex! We were sharing an amazing time together. We will always remember watching our new friends and these wonderful new families that were just beginning their lives together. Every day we watched as the trust grew in our children. All of us rooted for each other, hoping and praying all would go well through the rest of our adoptions process.

It was around this time, that Gregg and I decided on Olga's official name. They had encouraged us in many of our classes to let your child keep her birth name. This is often very special to the child later in life. We were reflecting on this advice and trying to decide whether or not to let Olga keep her birth name. We loved how the nurses said her name "Olya". We knew it would not be pronounced that way in English. In the Ukraine they say their "g"s like we say our "y's". Olga sounds more like "Olya", with the y sound sort of "rolling" off your tongue! The name Olga pronounced in Ukrainian sounds much prettier unfortunately than it sounds pronounced in English. One evening I said to Gregg, "what if we just drop the g and call her "Ola"? We agreed that this would sound familiar to her, close to what she was used to being called. This would be more or less just an "adaptation" of her name to work better with the English language. It was simple and sweet just like her! Luba and the nurses did not like this at all! We had to trust our own instincts though, and we started calling her Ola from then on and it felt right! Ola Ann Rietmann, we hoped and prayed, would become her official new name soon.

It was around this time I called home to talk with my Mom about our progress. My Mom could not wait to share with me the experience she had with my grandma that day. Apparently, when my mom told grandma exactly where we were in the Ukraine, much to my mothers surprise she announced that that was where her parents had come from. Not always being clear about our ancestor's roots, my grandmother pulled out a map that had a big red circle around Kiev. She said her parents were born in Germany and had fled from there during the war. The Ukraine was still part of Russia at that time. Many of the Germans went to work for what my grandma called the "Rich Russians"! As the War spread into Russia and her parents now being targeted as "traitors" by the German army, they were then forced to escape out of Russia via the Odessa Harbor. Zaporizhia is very close to Odessa. My great-grandfather managed to get a job on a cattle boat and hid my great-grandma down below with the cattle. This began their difficult journey into the Black Sea and eventually settling in Canada. My mom and I pondered over what unknown connection we might have to the Ukraine and the possibilities of it adding to the reason we were drawn back here to find our little girl! Again…. "How small the world really is"!!!!!!

One day we arrived early in the afternoon to the orphanage and some of the three and four-year-old children were out playing. As we walked toward the building we smiled and waved to the children. Suddenly one of the little boys broke away from his group and ran over and threw his arms around Gregg. He was a beautiful little boy. Blonde, blue-eyed, with his little baseball hat on backward, (I guess backward baseball hats on little boys is another universal thing!) Tears streamed down Gregg's face and mine. Gregg knelt down and hugged him for a long moment. I could tell that neither Gregg nor this precious little boy wanted to let go.

There are no words to describe how we felt. You do NOT want to let go of any of these beautiful children. You want to hold on and love them forever! Many of the other children followed at that point and we were surrounded by toddlers wanting hugs. We hugged them all, touched their sweet cheeks, and looked into their beautiful little eyes. We told them we loved them and prayed for them. It was very, very hard. It is probably a good thing the process to adopt is as difficult as it is. If it was easier and cheaper, I'm sure Gregg and I would have come home with at least a dozen children. Their precious little faces will be etched in our minds and haunt us forever. We think of them every day.

Things were coming together in terms of the legal aspect of our adoption. Luba was aggressive about getting our paperwork processed. When we were not at the orphanage with Ola, she dragged us all over to legal offices to file needed paperwork. The paperwork seemed to just keep coming and coming. Luba pleaded our case to have the thirty-day waiting period waived, stating that we had two children at home and a farm that was nearing harvest.

Luckily in the end this worked for us. Gregg and I were in total awe watching Luba at work. Often Luba signaled Gregg to help her "persuade" the government official to move our paperwork along in a timely manner! With out going into too much detail, I will just say that it "cost us" a time or two to have our legal documents done in a few hours rather than a few days! Everywhere we went she seemed to be "fighting" with the government officials. In the beginning this made us very nervous, but we grew to trust her tactics in the end. The way the Russian/Ukrainian language sounded to us was "short, choppy and abrupt"! Many times we thought Luba was fighting with someone only to have her tell us later that "we were just talking about the weather"! Another incident happened around this time which puzzled Gregg and I. When we went to apply for Ola's birth certificate, the clerk asked us where we would like Ola to be born? Confused we answered "Zaporizhia, where she was actually born". This really seemed to upset the clerk and Luba. "Don't you want us to put she was born in Ione, where you are from?" they asked. Apparently in the Ukraine most people do not tell their adopted children they are adopted. We tried to explain that we had entire community awaiting her arrival and that she would inevitably find out anyway. We never could make them understand that we would celebrate the unique and special way that Ola came into our family.

Luba arranged for us to have our first meeting with the judge. In the Ukraine you meet with the judge before your actual court date. This is when he will look over your paperwork, ask you questions, and decide if you are fit parents to adopt a Ukrainian child. This was an opportunity for the judge to get to know us. We were very nervous.

We met with the judge in his chambers at the courthouse for a fairly "casual" meeting. The judge ended up being very nice and the interview process went well. The judge wanted to know why we had chosen to adopt in the Ukraine. We explained the process that had led us there. We told him how much we admired the Ukrainian people for their strength and perseverance. We were impressed by how very proud and "independent" they were. We told him we could see how hard they worked. Gregg shared how he "related" to all the farmers and the fact the Ukraine is predominantly "agricultural." Gregg and the judge talked a lot about farming. Everywhere we go it ends up somehow being about farming, I thought to myself.

I told the judge how much I enjoyed the abundance of art and how impressed I was with all the talent the Ukrainian people seemed to have. The judge spoke fairly good English, but Natasha was there to translate also. At one point toward the end of our interview as we were preparing to leave, Natasha said something to the judge in Ukrainian that made him smile and blush. When we were out in the hall I asked her what she had said to him. She told me nonchalantly, "Oh, I just told him that I had not expected such a nice and very cute judge."

"Oh my God," I said, not able to hide my shock and amusement. "Here Gregg and I are absolute nervous wrecks and editing every word carefully that we say to the judge fearing we might offend him and YOU tell him he's CUTE!" "Oh, I'm so sorry," said Natasha. "Was that the wrong thing to do?"

She was very worried now that she had said something inappropriate that could affect our adoption.

Laughing, I told her not to worry.

"Well he WAS very nice and very cute," she said. We all laughed so hard we cried! It did a lot to relieve the tension.

"Who knows," I told her. "Maybe it helped."

Later that day, Luba informed us that our first meeting had gone very well with the judge and that our final court hearing had been set two days from then. In the Ukraine when you adopt, and you finally are able to get a court appointment, you rejoice. At that court date, the judge makes his decision and everything is final, right then and there. If your adoption is approved by the judge, the child becomes officially yours. Everything we had done to get to this point, and now finally the waiting, the worrying, the "heart aching" was almost over!

Two days seemed like an eternity, but we spent them going back and forth to the orphanage to play with our Ola. Luba still seemed to come up with more paperwork and offices to visit. Natasha and I spent a lot of time together. I had grown to love my new friend so much. I have the closest of friends and family at home, but I don't think I have ever had such deep, emotional, and spiritual conversations with anyone before. The "connection" Natasha and I made continues to amaze me. We held hands and talked for hours, all the while dreading the moment we would have to say good-bye.

Traditionally, along with a cash donation to the orphanage, most families buy a few things for the children. The nurses and caregivers start giving you wish lists from the moment you get there. After spending time with the children, most people are happy to buy them some of the things they need.

Gregg, Natasha, and I went shopping one day to pick up a few of the things on the wish lists they had given us. The caregivers were so excited and grateful when we brought back walkers, toys, and diapers. I did some shopping for Ola and had so much fun. This was when Gregg really began to panic as the realization of our having a daughter was starting to sink in. He'd ask, "But you already bought her a pair of shoes yesterday, didn't you dear?" "How many pairs of pajamas does she need honey?" "Yes, that is a darling dress and of course she needs it in pink AND blue." He was a very good sport and still is. He complains about my having too many shoes, but never about Ola's collection.

Our court date finally arrived! We showed up at the courthouse early and waited for our turn to enter the courtroom and have the judge make his final decision. He would also be deciding whether to waive our thirty-day waiting period. We sat with many of the other parents that we had gotten to know. Again, I am surprised how dirty and run down the court house is. There is not even a toilet, just a hole in the ground in an absolutely filthy small room.

One of the couples came out of the courtroom upset because they had found out that they would have to travel to another city in the Ukraine to obtain their child's original birth certificate before their adoption could be finalized. This would add at least another week to their adoption process.

Another couple we knew came out crying, but this time with joy as they had been awarded custody and their adoption was final. We were so happy for them. "Good luck," they said as we hugged them and told them good-bye. I don't think I can ever remember being more emotional and nervous. I was an absolute wreck while waiting, and the minutes ticked by so slowly. Ola is so much our baby girl by now that I can not imagine not taking her home.

Finally, it was our turn. My heart was pounding so hard I thought I might pass out. I was shaking and trying not to cry. The courtroom was dark and cold, lit only by the sunlight shining through the windows. I was struck by the large wooden cage off to one side, which I assume was for criminals they did not want to escape. It looked so medieval. The judge came in and we were all told to stand. Once again the judge and our attorney were all talking in Ukrainian and Natasha was trying her best to translate back and forth to us. I think Natasha was more nervous than we were. At one point the judge snapped at Natasha to "translate in a quicker manner," and "keep up with the procedure." Now she was really flustered.

There was a lady sitting behind me, and I wondered why she was there. I did not recognize her. She was asked to stand and the judge began to question her. I was very nervous about who she was and what she was saying. Later we would find out that the lady in the courtroom with us was the director from the Ministry of Education. The lady whom we had thought was so "cold" and "unfriendly" and who basically "scared us to death" had chosen to come and speak on our behalf. We found out that she rarely did this, but occasionally chose to speak for people who struck her as especially worthy of adopting a child from the Ukraine.

I'm still "blown away" by this. The way she had acted back at her office that first day we met her, I thought for some reason she hated us. After our adoption petition had been presented by our attorney, the judge asked us a few questions and we very nervously and respect-fully answered them. He then told us that he would be leaving the courtroom and going to his chambers to make his decision. We were asked to wait where we were. It seemed like forever while we waited. Gregg and I hugged each other and agreed we thought that things were going well! Natasha and I were freezing yet perspiring profusely. We squeezed each other's hands for comfort and encouragement. Natasha and Luba bonded strongly with our little Olga and with us, so this was emotional for them also. Natasha had said many times to me, "oooooh my goodness, I love this Olga." Then she would always add very seriously, "No, Sheraaal, I REALLY do LOVE this baby!"

Natasha shared with me that she had thought often that she might like to adopt also, but Ruslan did not want to. Ruslan did not think he could ever open up and love another child after losing their child the way they did. I felt so very sorry for them.

The door finally swung open from the chambers and the judge came back in. We all stood and faced him. Again, I thought I was going to throw up. He began to speak very seriously in Ukrainian, and Gregg and I anxiously waited for Natasha to interpret. "The judge has made his decision in this case," she said. More very serious Ukrainian talk; then Natasha looked at us and she choked up, tears streaming. Hardly able to speak, she interpreted the judge's words back to us with a big smile. "The child known as Kryla Olga Seregina will be allowed to be adopted by Gregg and Cheryle Rietmann."

Gregg and I immediately started to cry and tried our best to remain composed. The rest was all a blur of "legal lingo" back and forth. We were so happy and relieved. We were excused, and walking out of the courtroom we thanked the judge over and over again. The judge winked, smiled and said something in Ukrainian to Gregg, which Natasha had to interpret. He said, "Be patient with your daughter." "I will" Gregg answered, and again thanked the judge.

When we got out in the hallway we were all crying and hugging. Luba told us that the judge had agreed to waive our thirty-day waiting period. This added greatly to our joy. Ola was ours and in just a few more days we would be taking her and heading home to our boys.

"It's time for vodka now," exclaimed Luba, and we all were in complete agreement. It was definitely time to celebrate. We found a restaurant nearby. It was brand new and very modern. It was painted bright "hot" pink on the outside. They are not afraid to use "color" here in the Ukraine I thought. We all ordered drinks and began "toasting". We're all laughing and having fun when a rather large German Shepard came calmly up to our table. The server smiled, shrugged and said, "He is looking for treats from you". "Maybe you share your scraps with him later"; it is very common for dogs to wander in and out of the restaurants there. The people in the Ukraine hold their dogs in much higher regard than we do in America.

Luba began telling us what the next steps would be in completing our process. First, we would need to go get Ola and take her to a photo place that takes passport pictures. Luba had already started the legal paperwork needed to obtain her passport and her picture was all we needed to complete this step. This sounded easy but we would find out otherwise.

The pictures required for passports there have to be "perfect". Getting a fourteen month old to hold perfectly still and look directly at the camera proved to be quite a challenge. You need to get a front view and a side view and they both must be perfect.

Before we did the pictures, we needed to sign some more paperwork at the orphanage. The orphanage had told us to bring diapers, clothes, shoes, a coat and a hat. They are adamant about hats on babies in the Ukraine. They hand over your child pretty much "naked" from the orphanage. Ola would take nothing with her from her home of fourteen months, except maybe some vague images.

9

"Thank-you Zaporizhia"

We finished our lunch and "celebration" and headed for the orphanage. Luba told us that if all went well, it was possible she might be able to get us on the train and headed back to Kiev that night. We jumped in the taxi and headed back to our bed and breakfast to pack up our things and check out. We then headed back to the orphanage. We could not believe we were to this point and almost ready to head towards home. "Home", what a wonderful, beautiful place.

When we got back to the orphanage, it suddenly felt completely different to me. Why was MY daughter in this place? I just wanted them to give her to me NOW; she was officially mine now so just "hand her over".

We gave the nurse the new clothes we had bought Ola so she could go get her ready. "You are going home little one," we said to Ola. She was very unaware of the huge event that had just taken place in her life. She gave us a funny little smile, and off she went with the nurse rather unimpressed by all the commotion.

Luba offered to take Ola to the photography studio for us but my "mommy instincts" were pretty strong right now and I would not be handing my baby over to anyone not even Luba. I smiled and told Luba that I would go with her. We're really pressed for time now and after Ola was ready, we "hurriedly' headed off to get her pictures taken. As we hurried down the sidewalks and across the busy streets, I held Ola tightly. I was now even more aware of the "crazy drivers" the "drunks" and the "wild place" Zaporizhia is. Ola's eyes were huge as she looked around and clung to me.

I was getting so mad at all the people who kept bumping into us. I had gotten a little used to it by now, but not with my baby in my arms. We managed to get the pictures taken and then went back to the orphanage to wait, hoping they would turn out OK. Ola looked so cute in her new clothes, shoes, coat and hat! I had bought her bright shiny red shoes. Ola loved her new shoes and kept pointing at them proudly. The caregivers got such a kick out of Ola and her new red shoes.

We went to the director's office to sign the final paperwork. We heard that it was "customary" to make a "generous donation" to the orphanage if possible. We were happy to do this. We signed all the needed papers, made our donation, and waited to hear if the pictures had turned out for the passport. Luba had managed to get us on the evening train back to Kiev. All we were waiting for was Ola's passport. This was when Luba got the call that the passport pictures needed to be retaken; they were not acceptable. We of course were disappointed with this news! We were already cutting it really tight being able to get to the train on time, now it looked like it might be impossible. We might have to wait and leave tomorrow.

Part of our rush was because of the fact that we were approaching the weekend and the American embassy in Kiev is closed on the weekends. We still needed to get clearance at the embassy before we could leave the country with Ola. We had hoped not to spend the weekend in Kiev.

We raced back to the photo shop and redid the pictures. We crossed our fingers and hoped they would turn out and that maybe we would still make the train that night. We went back and again "anxiously" waited at the orphanage. Ola seemed ready to go too. She marched around proudly in her new red shoes. One of the caregivers told us how "lucky we were to get Olya", "she is such a good girl", she said.

The caregivers had tears in their eyes and we could tell it was hard for them to say good-bye to Olga. Natasha told me that the caregivers said they were so happy Ola had found such a "nice young mommy". This made me smile, especially about the "young" part! Finally, we got the news that the pictures came out OK, for the passport. Luba ran back to pick up the passport and we were on our way.

Leaving the orphanage with Ola felt wonderful! It was almost "surreal" as we walked down the long, dark hallway and out into the bright sunlight. "Say good-bye to your home of the last fourteen months, I said to Ola". "I am grateful they took such good care of you until I could get to you."

Once again we all piled into the tiny taxi and drove like crazy to the train station on time. We were not sure if we would make it. You had to check in twenty minutes before departure time or you would not be permitted to board. We had no car seat (no one does in the Ukraine) so I was an absolute nervous wreck in the taxi holding Ola tightly in my arms. With Ola in the car, we are especially uncomfortable about the "insane" way they drive in the Ukraine. I prayed the whole time we were in the car. "Please, after all of this, just let us get home safe and sound."

We made it to the train station and as we unloaded and paid the taxi driver, Luba ran ahead to see if we still had tickets waiting for us. Luckily we did. We would be heading back to Kiev that night. Luba explained that Yuri was working on getting us an appointment with the INS the next day, and if our luck held out we might be heading home over the weekend. We couldn't believe how wonderful that sounded.

Gregg, Ola, Luba, Natasha, and I sat waiting for the call for passengers to begin boarding the train. I was so anxious to get on the train and head back to Kiev but also had a sick feeling in my stomach anticipating having to tell Natasha good-bye. We both were dreading it. The tears were already there, the lumps in our throats growing. We put it off as long as we could. We played with Ola in the station and enjoyed watching her laugh and smile. Ola had already come so far in the last few weeks.

Ola had gotten to know Natasha pretty well, so she went to her easily. Natasha hugged and kissed her and told her what a "good life" she was going to have. "I will be at your wedding," she told Ola.

We kept reminding Natasha of the important part she had played in our getting Ola and how we could not have done it without her." We will make sure to tell her all about her "Aunt Natasha," we promised. "We will tell her all you did for us!" "I just can't believe how much I love her," Natasha kept saying.

"She loves you too," we told her.

Gregg thanked Natasha repeatedly as they hugged and said farewell. Natasha and I finally realized we could not put off our good-bye any longer. How do you say good-bye to someone you have fallen so in love with and know you will probably never see again? There were no words, but our eyes said it all.

In America, we take the freedom we have to travel for granted. We can travel anywhere we want to, anytime we want to, but this is not the case in the Ukraine. In the Ukraine it is very, very difficult to get a visa out of the country. It is almost impossible. Especially when you are as "valuable" as Natasha is. With Natasha being a teacher of English at a university, they would not want to lose her. They do not take the risk of allowing their people to travel for the fear they may not return. This is a justified concern, as living in the Ukraine must be very difficult. We all want the best lives for ourselves and our families so I would imagine it would be quite tempting to try to find a better and easier life somewhere else.

I did not imagine that Gregg and I would be very anxious to return to the Ukraine. Therefore, with our reluctance about returning and the poor odds Natasha ever being able to visit us, we knew this was really good-bye. There was a slight possibility Natasha would someday be able to travel a little more freely around Europe, so someday we could meet there somewhere. "I will find a way to make it to Ola's wedding though," Natasha told me firmly.

We decided, we simply could not, would not, say good-bye. We came up with a plan. We agreed we would meet in Paris someday. We started with the plan of meeting in Paris in 10 years, but this did not stop the tears. We brought it all the way down to meeting in Paris in 1 year, thinking that pretending this "COULD" happen that it might somehow help us gain some composure! Eventually we realized nothing would make our good-bye any easier. We were not going to keep our hearts from breaking, so with tears streaming, we held each other tightly for as long as we could. Natasha finally pulled back, touched my face, our eyes still searching for the words. We finally managed weak smiles and Natasha turned and walked away. She knew she could not look back.

I will never forget how hard it was to watch her walk away. Isn't it amazing how some people can come into your lives and change you forever? "All aboard," we heard over the speakers. It was time to load the train. Good-bye Zaporizhia, I thought. You have given us life's most precious and beautiful gift. Thank you!

Natasha holding Ola, while Luba feeds her

We boarded the train with Ola's eyes still great big and looking all around. "Your life with us is about to begin," I said. "This is just the first of many adventures we will have together!"

Luba was scolding me again, and wanting to know where Ola's hat was. Luba was really getting on my nerves! Gregg got all of our luggage onto the train. Again, I'm feeling guilty about my inability to pack light as I watch him lugging my large suitcase around! We settled into our sleeping car, excited about the fact that we were starting our journey home with our daughter. The last hoop we had to jump through was getting clearance from the INS in Kiev. We weren't too worried about this and Yuri was supposed to be working on getting us an appointment.

We talked about our trip down on this train and how different we were feeling compared to how we were feeling now! We were so fearful of the unknown on the way to Zaporizhia and now we were so very happy and relieved to have our beautiful little girl with us. Everything had worked out better than we ever could have imagined. We never dreamed we would find such a perfect baby girl to call our own.

Ola would still not go to Gregg without crying, but I wasn't complaining. I wasn't tired of holding her yet! She felt so natural and meant to be in my arms! Occasionally I had to go to the bathroom, so Ola was forced to go to Gregg. Once I was out of sight Ola did fine with Gregg, so that was good. She was getting less and less leery of him. I told her I wasn't sure about him at first either, but that she would soon fall in love with him like I did.

We had some dinner on the train. Ola and I shared some pureed potatoes. I ordered white wine and got red wine again, but I was happy with whatever I got. Wine is wine.

Soon we were ready for some sleep. We were exhausted. I was wondering how Ola and I were going to sleep on that narrow seat together without one of us falling off. We all began to settle down and Ola started to yawn and look very sleepy. As Luba got ready to head back to her own sleeping car she kissed Ola and told her goodnight. Ola looked up at Luba, pointed to me, and said, "Mamma!" All of us squealed with surprise and delight. This was the first time she had called me Mamma! I was laughing and crying at the same time.

She called me Mamma from that moment on. As I said before, I don't think I will ever take having this little girl calling me Mamma for granted. I still melt.

"I will work hard to remain worthy of being your Mamma, my sweet baby girl," I told her.

Ola slept contentedly in my arms all night. I managed to doze off and on in our cramped little quarters. I would wake up and look down on Ola as the moonlight shone through the window on her pretty little face. I woke up one time and looked over to see Gregg awake and looking at us and the moon. "Did you notice the moon?" he whispered. "Yes," I answered. "It is a gorgeous full moon!" This was when we realized the amazing coincidence, that both our boys were born on a full moon and now here on the first night that Ola was officially ours, there was a full moon. We smiled at each other and said, "Wow!" I do not know what shone brighter in that little train car, the love that the three of us shared or the perfect full moon. We couldn't help but take this as a sign from God above. We knew he must be pleased and that we had his blessing. We felt very grateful.

We woke up early to the sun shining in on us now. I was surprised that Ola slept so well; she didn't fuss once. We were excited to get back to Kiev and anxious to hear if Yuri was able to get us an appointment at the INS. He did not think he would have any problems. There was even a chance we would get through INS and on a plane home that night, tomorrow at the latest.

Luba came to our car to check on us and had a present for Ola. She had bought her some keepsakes from Zaporizhia. Luba had bought a wooden plaque with a picture of a Cossack hand painted on it. On the back of it she had signed her name. "Luba, means love," she told Olga. We had not known that until now. We thought that was very sweet. We really admired Luba, she could be a tough attorney one minute, and in the next moment be such a sweet and caring person.

We shared some espresso with Luba and told her how much we appreciated her help. She understood the words "thank you" which we said over and over to her. Luba pointed to Gregg, me and Ola in a circular motion and then to her heart and said, "Thanks enough!"

We all got off the train,(yes, the loud disco music was blaring) and began looking for Jenya. Jenya was supposed to be waiting for us. Alas, there was no Jenya to be found so Luba hailed a taxi for us. Luba would take us to a hotel and get us settled and "turn us back over to Yuri." Luba's work would be done for us at this point.

Luba looked very tired and ready to go home. I admired the fact that Luba had brought only a small overnight bag and had managed to get through almost two weeks in Zaporizhia with that. She had worn the same suit the whole time. Gregg told me I could learn from this.

Back in Kiev we checked into a nice hotel and got a nice-sized room. We took it for only one night as we hoped we would need only one night! Again, this was a difficult good-bye and it was so hard to convey our gratitude. Luba had been amazing! We now understood what Yuri had meant by "a good attorney for the difficult regions." She really had come through for us.

We had a hard time getting in touch with Yuri and we were getting very anxious about when our appointment time was with the INS. We got to our room and I was ready for Ola and me to have a bath. Ola screamed "bloody murder" when I put her in the tub. She was absolutely terrified of this "large body of water" we were immersing her in. We immediately assumed that Olga had not had many baths, at least not in a great big tub like this one. It felt good to get her all cleaned up though. She was now all sweet-smelling with baby powder and lotions and, of course, some new pajamas. I then turned Ola over to Gregg so that I could bathe. The water in Kiev was at least not quite as brown as it had been in Zaporizhia. Ola still screamed when I gave her to Gregg, but obviously she was going to have to get used to him, and I was really looking forward to a nice hot relaxing bath.

After we had all freshened up we finally reached Yuri. Unfortunately, we had another problem on our hands. The INS had lost our paperwork. They had nothing on file for us. Recently, in only the last few months, the INS had started processing all Ukrainian adoptions in Kiev rather that Warsaw, Poland. This was great because before, we would have had to travel to Poland to complete our adoption process.

The fact that they had no file on us sent us straight into panic. I very specifically remembered having transferred our files to Kiev. For some reason, even though they started processing adoptions in Kiev, they still first went to Poland and then had to be transferred to Kiev.

We made what seemed like a hundred phone calls back and forth to the INS in Poland and the INS in Kiev, and both offices were blaming the other. Poland swore to us that they had sent them and suggested we contact FedEx. Kiev said they never received them! Tracking down our file could take days, and putting together a new "certifiable" file could take days also.

Yuri threw his hands in the air and said that we would have to take care of this ourselves. There was nothing more he could do until we got this straightened out. The INS would only talk to us not him. We couldn't believe this was happening. We thought this was going to be the last, easy step in finishing up and getting home. This could take days, maybe weeks, to straighten out. I broke down and cried. I went back and forth from being furious to crying.

To make matters worse we came to find out that this particular Friday, happened to be a Ukrainian Holiday. All the government offices were either closed or working with limited staff. We were devastated, but finally realized we would not be going home until Monday at the soonest and that would be if we were lucky and tracked down our lost file.

We were missing our boys so much by now. At least we had our beautiful little girl with us though, and that helped a great deal. We would be spending the weekend in Kiev and decided to settle into our hotel room and make the best of it. Ola loved running up and down the hallways and in the lobby. She was becoming less and less leery of Gregg, but still clung to me most of the time. Occasionally I would need a break and have to give her to Gregg and go for a walk outside or at the mall next door. One time I came back from a walk and found Gregg and Ola fast asleep together in a chair. With Ola on Gregg's chest, they were both snoring loudly!

Gregg and I laughed about the level of service in the hotel. Sometimes you would pick up the phone and order room service and someone would cheerfully take your order and it would be brought to your room, no problem. Next time you would pick up the phone to order room service and be told sternly that there was no room service.

Upstairs was a restaurant, wine bar, espresso bar, and disco. Sometimes you could go there and order coffee, wine, or food to take back to your room and they would gladly accommodate you. At other times they would glare at you and say, "No take back to room!" I guess it depended on who you asked and what kind of mood they were in. Many mornings I would go to the espresso bar upstairs for coffee, and find the employees sleeping in the booths or at the tables.

As I said before, the shifts they work in the Ukraine are much different than in America. The same employees would be there for days in the same clothes, and by the end of the weekend, they were understandably very crabby. By the looks of some of them in the mornings, I think they may have "partied" with the customers too! I decided, after a few "scary" mornings, not to take a chance on the espresso bar too early in the mornings. In the evenings I would order a Vodka tonic and if I was able to take it back to the room, it would last me for days. The drinks are very tall and strong there. I would call and ask for more tonic and "beg" for more ice. Ice is a "luxury" there, again I assume because of the lack of refrigeration. Gregg ordered Budweiser one night. He received a beer in a Budweiser bottle, but the beer tasted much different than the Budweiser tastes in the USA.

I purchased some peanuts once thinking "surely peanuts are peanuts," but oh my goodness, I was wrong again. I could not believe how awful they tasted. I could not eat them. I looked at the ingredients and they were roasted in pork fat. Everything in the Ukraine is cooked in pork fat.

Staying in a hotel room with a fourteen-month-old for very long is not much fun! We didn't have many toys or much to entertain her with. We didn't have much to entertain ourselves with either. The only thing on TV in English was CNN and we grew sick of the news. We did have fun for a while watching American movies in Ukrainian. Picture Bill Murray talking Russian, of course, Bill Murray is funny no matter what.

We were having fun getting to know our new baby, but the four walls would close in on us from time to time. One evening we decided to take Ola and dine up in the restaurant (disco) upstairs. I was a little worried about Ola and the very loud music and the fact the bar is all together in the same large room, but we really needed to get out of our room.

We started out pretty well. We ordered our dinner and Gregg and I had a nice glass of red wine. Our dinner came and Ola was being so good. We were managing to have a nice, calm, relaxing evening. About then, as usual, the very loud disco music came on. The lights were dimmed and the huge mirror ball started to spin. I was afraid Ola would be frightened.

At first she clung to me and stared at the shiny, spinning ball. Then she wanted down. She started to throw an absolute fit, so I let her out of the booth and hoped she would be happy playing close to our table. No such luck! Ola kept pulling on my leg and crying, and I was thinking maybe she wanted to leave. Reluctantly I got up and tried to make her happy so Gregg could finish his meal. To my surprise, Ola grabbed my hand and dragged me to the dance floor. It was early in the evening so no one was dancing. Much to our amazement and shock Ola started shaking her little "booty" and dancing to the music! It was as if she had been out dancing at the disco many times. Our shy, timid little girl was suddenly quite the performer. We did not realize she was a dancer, and quite a dancer at that.

Gregg and I laughed so hard. It was so cute. We spent the rest of the evening dancing at the disco with Ola. Boy, could she boogie. We never saw her so happy. We had so much fun, but Gregg and I wore out long before Ola did. We dragged her back to our room. She was upset about the party ending so soon, but we all slept well that night!

We made it through the weekend and woke up early Monday morning determined to solve the problem of our lost documents. Again, we began making phone calls. Each phone call we made seemed to lead us down the road to nowhere, and it was causing me to become more and more angry and frustrated. Luckily, we finally got a nice woman who seemed to sympathize with our plight and took on our case. She was going to "find out what had happened to our file one way or another"! We hung up after talking with her feeling a little better about the fact that at least someone was going to bat for us.

Within about an hour the nice woman called back and had found our file. It had been misfiled. All this problem and waiting because Rietmann had been filed under Reitmann, (i before e I thought, filing is "underrated"!)

With our file finally located, we were then transferred to a man who would be making us an appointment with the INS. We were told that we could have an appointment on Thursday. Gregg repeated the information to me, discouraged, (Thursday being 4 days away!) This was when I lost my temper and snatched the phone from Gregg's hand. With my voice quite raised, I explained to the nice man that we "WOULD" be seen "TODAY OR TOMORROW." It was not OUR fault our file had been MISPELLED and MISFILED and that we had already spent an extra FOUR DAYS waiting because of this error. It was really not FAIR or REASONABLE to ask us to spend another four days waiting.

Luckily, my temper tantrum did not backfire and the nice man responded by saying, "Tomorrow at 10:00 a.m. then?" "Thank-you," I said politely and hung up the phone. "Whew," Gregg said, relieved that my speaking to the Ukrainian government official in such a tone had not worked against us. We had an appointment to finish up with the INS the next day. Yuri said he was 99 percent sure we would zip through the INS and should be ready to fly home early Wednesday morning.

Because of the time difference we were actually ahead a day so this would put us home Tuesday night, June 16, which happened to be my mom's birthday. I phoned my mom and told her that we would be coming home and bringing her a wonderful birthday present, a new granddaughter! We called the boys and told them "only one more day" and we would be home. It was starting to be so "painful" to hear their precious little voices on the phone and not be able to hold them. My heart ached for them. We missed them so much.

We headed for the INS the next morning. All of our paperwork was in order and ready to go. We caught a taxi and got to the INS by 10:00 a.m. There was a huge line and people were gathered all around the INS building. We were alarmed and worried at the thought of having to wait in that line with a fourteen-month old. As we got out of the taxi, a guard came over and asked, "Are you Americans?" "Yes," we answered. "Go ahead of the crowd and go on in," he told us. We were so relieved to be heading to the front of the line and the hundreds of people waiting. Most of the people waiting were people who needed clearance for their new brides or fiancés. They were applying for visas to leave the Ukraine. We learned there were many men who took advantage of the women in the Ukraine and their strong desire to get out of the country. There are many "mail order" or "arranged" "marriages" made via the Internet or mail. Many of the women hardly knew the men they would be marrying but were willing to take a chance on them as they were anxious, sometimes desperate, to find a better life. The taxi driver was nice and said he would come back in one hour. After we went through the normal security checks we were directed into a room full of Americans getting clearance from the INS. It was comforting being in a room with people who spoke English. Most of the people were families adopting. It was fun to hear each family's story. Many of the families were people who had returned to adopt more children. Whenever people try to give Gregg and I too much credit for everything we went through to adopt Ola, we have to shake our heads and tell them about all the people we met who had adopted several children from the Ukraine and all over the world. So many people have made so many trips and accrued so much debt in order to adopt these beautiful, deserving children. We had barely been able to endure one trip.

It is funny how similar adoption is to childbirth in the way you swear while you're going through it, that you would NEVER do it again, but after a little time goes by, you forget the hardship and say, "Oh, it wasn't THAT bad. I could do it again." Especially after you've seen and experienced the wonderful results. There are so many amazing, generous people who adopt entire families so that siblings can stay together. There are also those who are willing to take on children with huge medical problems, without hesitation. It takes great faith to do this. These are the people who should really be applauded. Their hearts are huge and they are brave, unselfish people. God bless them all! We can see how it would be addicting though. When you get home and experience all the joy these children bring to your life, you just want to go back and embrace all the beautiful children who need homes. We saw so many, perfect, beautiful children and as I've said many times, "If I was a little younger, a little richer, I'd probably have to go back!" We met some people at the INS who were from Corvallis, Oregon. We learned that people from the State of Oregon adopt more children than anyplace else in the world! We thought that was so cool! "Way to go Oregon!" We met a family from Oregon who had adopted four children from the Ukraine. On this trip they had come back for a thirteen-year-old girl they had met on one of their trips before. The young girl had the biggest smile on her face. You could tell she was so happy to finally have a family. I was impressed with how good she was with the younger children who were two, four and seven.

We ended up being on the same flight home with them. The thirteen-year-old, newly adopted girl never quit smiling. She held each of her new younger brothers and sister on her lap and helped care for them as if she'd been doing it forever. She took them to the bathroom, shared her food, and did all the "normal" things older sisters do. It was so heart warming. I kept watching her and smiling.

We got through the INS in Kiev fairly painlessly. Everything was signed, stamped, and authorized for the last time in the Ukraine and would not need to be stamped again until we got to the INS in America. We could take Ola back to the United States and HOME. The taxi was waiting for us when we came out and he took us back to the hotel. Yuri had gotten us on a very early flight the next morning. We arranged for this nice taxi driver to pick us up at 4:30 the next morning. We went back to our room and began packing. We realized that because of the extra things we needed for Ola and also with the souvenirs we had purchased, that we had way too much stuff to try and get on the plane and home. We decided to leave some of our things. We left a huge pile of clothing and personal items in our room. I had been wearing some of the clothes for two weeks straight and never wanted to see them again anyway. We hoped the maids might be happy to have them. Yuri phoned and wanted to stop by to say good-bye and meet Ola. He brought us some Ukrainian wine as a gift. We thanked Yuri over and over for everything he had done for us. We gave him lots of big hugs. We had a nice relaxing evening, but it was hard to sleep because we were so excited to be going home the next day. We called home so everyone knew we were finally on our way back to them. Many of them would be waiting for us at the Pasco Airport. Gregg and I were so excited to see the boys we could hardly stand it.

We were ready to go and went down to the lobby at 4:30 a.m. sharp. Our taxi was waiting, so we checked out and headed to the airport. We got to the airport two hours before our flight left, but Gregg was so nervous about missing the flight that he insisted we get there early. We had some breakfast and played with Ola in the terminal. Ola was wide-awake and raring to go so Gregg and I took turns chasing her. We were happy to see some of the same people we had seen at the INS who were also heading home. Everyone was so happy. As we went through clearance to board the plane, everyone made over Ola. The staff and all the people boarding seemed to be aware that we had a newly adopted daughter. Everyone was congratulating us. As we went through the security checks at the airport, we were asked the regular questions like, "Do you have any items that are perishable, explosive?" "Have you left your baggage unattended?" "Has anyone given you anything that you did not have control of?" I'm saying, "No, no, no." Gregg at this point, for some reason, seemed to have the need to tell the agent about the wine Yuri had given us the night before. We had packed it in a box for carry-on; thinking is might break if we checked it. Suddenly I heard Gregg saying, "Well, we do have this Ukrainian wine…I mean, I GUESS it's just wine…I don't really know for sure!" I wasn't sure if Gregg was being funny, but neither the clerk nor I thought he was being funny at all. We had been told not to take anything questionable on the plane, and that sometimes they wouldn't even allow baby food. I was glaring now at my husband, and saying with my eyes and every part of my being, "SHUT UP GREGG!" I was also really nervous this would be a problem and cause a delay in our boarding.

Luckily, the clerk shrugged and told us to go on ahead and board, he was sure the wine was no problem. As soon as we were around the corner I said to Gregg, "So we are FINALLY boarding the plane to go home and you decide to be funny with the clearance clerk about some stupid wine we are taking on the plane?" Gregg admitted that maybe his timing was poor and that it might not have been that funny. Holding Ola and shaking my head in disbelief we finally boarded the plane and were headed home to the U.S.

Our plane ride home went pretty well. Ola was, for the most part, a very good girl. I admit I had given her just a little bit of Benadryl in hopes we both might get a little sleep. Everyone on the plane was totally enamored with our little Ola! Our adoption story had spread throughout the entire plane so everyone kept saying things like, "Great job," or "Good for you guys," and "She is so beautiful!" As I chased Ola up and down the aisle people would reach out and squeeze my hand with approval. We got lots of winks and "way to go" smiles. It seemed as if everyone we talked to had an adoption story. "I was adopted," or "a sister, aunt, or best friend was adopted," or "we adopted two children also." One man had adopted five children! A mother and her adopted daughter sat right behind us on the plane. The young daughter played with Ola the whole way home, which helped entertain her immensely. Adoption seems to open up a whole new world to you that you were never aware of before. You suddenly see and hear adoption stories everywhere!

Despite all the nice people we traveled with, it was still a very long trip home. It was over twelve hours, and we did have some stressful moments. Ola would still not go to Gregg very easily. He occasionally would just have to take her so I could go to the restroom or walk around and stretch my legs. If I was out of sight, she did OK, so occasionally I would go hide around the corner, just to give my arms a break!

When we landed in Seattle Gregg and I were so happy and relieved. We were home in America. Little did we realize that until you go through immigrations in Seattle, you are not treated like an American. You are shuttled directly off the plane to an INS clearance area where a painfully slow government process begins to clear you, yet again, for reentry into the USA. I think I was a little out of practice in the "baby" area, as I had not packed enough diapers. Also, a jar of baby food had broken inside the diaper bag and had soaked the diapers and change of clothes I did have for Ola. By the time we landed in Seattle, I had no diapers, no juice or food left. I felt like a total "loser mom". We were exhausted and "stressed to the max." We were feeling "so close," yet "so far" from home.

It took (literally) hours to get through the INS in Seattle. We were very worried we would miss our connecting flight to Pasco. We decided right away that we would rent a car, catch a bus, whatever we needed to do, but we would be HOME TONIGHT!

Apparently there had been a "change of protocol" with the manner in which "adoption procedures" were handled in Seattle and "the new guy" did not know how to process our paperwork. Ola was soaked and I "begged" them to let me just "zip" around the corner to the gift shop to buy some diapers, juice, and maybe a tee shirt or something to change Ola into. I did understand why they could not let me do that, but I was "desperate". There was a moment when Ola and I sat on the "cold linoleum" floor and both cried. (There were no chairs left, as immigration was very crowded that day!) Gregg felt helpless.

We were finally back home in the U.S. and this was turning out to be one of the hardest parts of our trip. We were treated no differently than any of the other "foreigners" we were there with. We finally got clearance and were released to re-enter the country, free to continue on to our final destination. Gregg told me to take Ola and head to the gate where we would catch the plane to Pasco. Gregg had to take off in a "dead run" to claim our luggage and re-check it onto our plane to Pasco. Because we had been in another country, we could not have our luggage checked automatically from Kiev to Pasco. It was going to be very tight time-wise, and I wished Gregg "good luck". I ran to the nearest gift shop and found diapers, apple juice, and a small tee shirt for Ola. Ola and I could not have been more thrilled with the twelve-month size Seattle Mariners tee shirt. I whipped into the nearest bathroom, cleaned Ola up, and dashed to our departing gate. As I was going up the escalator, I could see the floor below us and saw Gregg running with all our bags, sweating and panting.

"Go honey," I called out. I wasn't sure whether to laugh or cry at this point. Ola and I were anxiously waiting at the departure gate when Gregg barely arrived on time. Gregg had told me before to "get on that plane, with or without me", but I did not want to have to do that. Mission accomplished; our bags had been checked. Gregg said that to make matters worse, the elevator was either taking forever or was broke down, so Gregg in a panic with all our heavy luggage had had to take the stairs. It was very close, but we had made it and were boarding our final plane for home. I cannot tell you how happy and relieved we were. I had not been able to get Ola to sleep very much the entire trip home, but, of course, on the plane from Seattle to Pasco, Ola falls asleep. I knew Ola was going to probably just get to sleep and then be woken up when we got into Pasco. She was most likely not going to be in the best mood when we landed. I was a little worried about having a "cranky" baby, and that this would be her first meeting with her new brothers, family, and friends. It would be overwhelming for her and I had hoped she would have had a good nap and be in a good mood. I should know by now that things never go that perfectly. It was still going to be a wonderful reunion though, "cranky baby" or not. When we landed in Pasco and got off the plane, it was a beautiful, sunny day. My parents, Gregg's dad, Stacie, and the boys were there waiting. My dad was holding a huge sign he had made himself that said, "Welcome Ola." Stacie captured a picture of me holding Ola and reaching for the boys with tears in my eyes, trying not to lose it. The picture speaks a thousand words about all the emotions we were feeling! I've never been happier than I was at that moment. Holding my boys and my daughter in my arms, I wished for nothing more than what I had right there. Gregg joined us in our family hug feeling the same way I did. We were so grateful for this moment. To finally be home, our family complete. The boys said their first hello's to Ola. They kept saying, "She's so cute!" Everyone else wanted hugs also. We were all so overwhelmed with emotion. Everyone tried to "hang back" a little to let the boys and us embrace. We couldn't even begin to tell the boys how very much we had missed them. Evan kept saying over and over how glad he was that we were home and how much he missed us. Tanner, being the "cool one", sheepishly admitted that he didn't think he would miss us, but he did. "A lot more than I thought I would," he confessed. Ola was a little overwhelmed by the welcoming committee and clung pretty tightly to me. After an emotional reunion, we pulled ourselves together and headed toward the car. We waited outside for Gregg to get our luggage again, thankfully for the last time! My mom told me later that a woman had come up to her at the airport and pointing to us said, "What a pretty baby," and then added, "Gee, she sure looks like her Mamma." My mom, of course, could not resist telling her the whole story about our just returning from the Ukraine and that we had just adopted Ola. The lady was amazed.

Home at last, reaching for my boys

An emotional family reunion

We finally made it into our Suburban and headed towards home. The boys were starving so we went through a McDonald's drive through window. Ola would have her first taste of real American food. She loved the French fries. I enjoyed them also, because they were not fried in pork fat. I couldn't believe how much better McDonald's tastes is the U.S. My sisters had reluctantly agreed to give us just a day or two to get settled before they visited and met Ola. This had been something our adoption agency had strongly suggested. In retrospect I wish they had all been at the airport to greet us. I am so close to my sisters and I would have loved to have had them there to share our arrival home. They would have all cried though, and then I would have cried more, so maybe it was best they weren't there. My sister, Missy, seemed to have the hardest time waiting. She called on my cell phone on our way home and begged to meet us somewhere "on the road" so that they could meet Ola. We met at our common meeting place, "the gravel pit." Missy and her husband, Todd, along with my niece and nephew, Maddie and Jake, anxiously awaited. We pulled in and they ran to the car. Maddie and Jake had made adorable little cards for Ola. They all oohed and aahed about how cute she was. Ola was not sure about all the attention she was getting, but it was fun for all of us to get to see each other and share in our joy.

We were exhausted though and ready to be home, so we kept it short. We had planned a family BBQ in a few days where everyone would get to spend time with Ola and get to know her better. Poor Ola was just going to have to get used to being in a very large and close family, probably sooner rather than later. There was not going to be anyway to keep the troops away for long. When we pulled up to the house there were balloons everywhere. Family and friends had tied balloons and hung "Welcome Home, Ola" signs all over, inside and outside our house. Ola loved the balloons!

No words can describe how good it was to be home. Tears of joy streamed freely for both Gregg and I. Stacie couldn't wait for us to get in the house and show us her surprise. She and my sister, Missy, had painted and decorated Ola's room so beautifully. When Gregg and I left to go to the Ukraine, we had thought we would be getting a toddler, so we had left a little girl's room ready, not a nursery for a baby. After we realized we were getting Ola, I had called my sister, Missy, and asked her if she could get a crib set up for us before we got home. Little did I know they would go to this much trouble. They painted Ola's bedroom a beautiful light lavender color, with cream-colored stars in the corners. A darling fairy hung from the ceiling. Her crib was all made up, pictures were hung, and beautiful quilts were everywhere. It was a perfect, magical room that had been put together with lots of love. This, of course, pushed Gregg and me over the edge and there was really no holding back the tears. Stacie left with us having no idea how to thank her enough. We didn't know how to thank all the many people who had helped out in so many ways while we were gone.

We all ended up in Gregg's and my bedroom. We cuddled and kissed all together for a while. Our whole family was all together snuggly, safe, and warm. Luckily Ola and the rest of us all fell asleep easily. Asleep at home in our own beds. Home, sweet home.

10

"Home Sweet Home"

As I finished typing this story, referring back to my journal almost a year after getting home with Ola, I reflect back fondly. The first few months home with Ola were not always easy. It was a happy and fun time though and Ola adjusted very well. We had read so many stories about children who had had a very hard time adjusting once their families got them home. We knew we were lucky that Ola did so well.

At first, it was hard because I could not go anywhere or do anything without Ola crying. I could not walk out of the room without her screaming. Luckily, Ola took to my sisters amazingly well. She would go to them and not cry. If I handed her to a sister, I could sneak around the corner somewhere and then she'd be fine with them. Maybe my sisters look enough like me and have similar enough mannerisms that she feels as comfortable and safe with them as she does with me.

I call my sisters Ola's "co-mammas." Ola loves her aunts so much and I never feel bad about leaving her with them although they spoil her rotten. It was a little suffocating at times for me at first, like I had grown another appendage. We had to be connected at all times, but we survived. She got better and better with time as she began to feel more secure. I had a couple of young girls come help me with housework and play with Ola so that I could get a break. She only wanted me at first though, and there were definitely days that I thought I might go a little crazy.

Ola gradually grew as comfortable with Gregg as she was with me. Her preference has definitely changed now. At this point, she is totally a Daddy's girl. The boys are awesome big brothers and were from day one. They are so patient and understanding with her. There have been times when I felt bad for not being able to give them as much time or attention, because all of my time and energy was going toward Ola. They never complained though.

We had Ola's christening at my sister's cabin in the mountains by Lake Pendland. It was beautiful. It was a day to "officially" welcome Ola into our family, and also a time to reaffirm our appreciation for all of our family. I wrote the ceremony to include all of the children. I had Tanner and Evan and Ola's cousin gather around the fireplace as the snow fell softly outside.

Ola wore a cream-colored dress with fur around the bottom and collar. She also had a matching hat and boots with fur on them. She pranced around proudly all day in her beautiful christening gown! In the ceremony I asked everyone to try to share "a little bit of themselves" with Ola, as they each had something uniquely their own to teach her. I asked that they all help watch over Ola and each other over the years.

We had multi-colored roses to represent love, hope, peace, and friendship. They each gave one to Ola. It was a special day for us. I told my sister that having Ola and watching her with our family was just like I dreamed it would be. This was definitely a time to celebrate family and friends.

Ola's christening and "family appreciation day!"

"From no family to lots of family"!

Rietmann family

Turner family

After the first year of being home with Ola, we have settled in and gotten back to being your basic, normal American family. I unfortunately have never been very good at staying home though. I've never wanted to be a housewife. As I suspect it is with most women, I just do not find housework to be the slightest bit rewarding. God bless stay-at-home moms, for it truly is the hardest job on earth.

For the first few months I rarely left Ola. Then, as I said before, I found a babysitter I trusted and my family helped out so that I could get away more. Now that Ola has adjusted and is a very normal two-year-old, we have begun moving forward with our lives. Ola has gotten to be quite a social butterfly at this point, and she is not that happy being home (with just Mom) everyday either. She has a wonderful group of friends her age and is much happier having someone to play with.

We are blessed to have a very special young lady who watches Ola often. Niki is part of our extended family. Ola calls her "Neenee" and absolutely adores her! I tell Niki that God knew I needed a little help, so he sent her to me, and I am so grateful! Because of Niki, I am able to start taking a little bit of my own life back.

I've read in books and been told by other adoptive parents that often there is a defining moment when you realize beyond a shadow of a doubt that the child you have adopted is absolutely your own. This moment came for us because of a terribly frightening moment and a phone call from Niki.

I was at home working on a project and had taken Ola into Niki, where she was also babysitting for friends of ours. Apparently Ola and her little friend Morgan were doing summersaults. Ola came down rather hard on her back and knocked the wind out of herself. She got up crying really hard and ran to Niki. When Niki picked her up Ola seemed to be having trouble breathing. Ola's eyes rolled back in her head and she went unconscious. According to Niki, Ola then turned blue and began convulsing. Luckily after a few seconds (which seemed like days to Niki), Ola began breathing. Obviously, Niki was very shaken up about this apparent seizure and it scared her to death.

I knew immediately when I heard Niki's voice on the phone that something was terribly wrong. She told me what had happened and I told her we would be right there. I got a hold of Gregg and we rushed into get her and take her to the hospital. Gregg and I were so scared. After the doctors examined her and ran some tests at our local hospital, they referred us to a neurologist in Bend, Oregon. In Bend, Ola had an EEG, blood work, and a thorough exam. The doctors there all came to the same conclusion that Ola had most likely knocked the wind out of herself and that added to her crying so hard it caused her to lose consciousness. Apparently this series of events can cause or lead to a seizure.

The doctors found nothing they felt they needed to be concerned with. No brain abnormalities, such as epilepsy or anything like that showed up on the EEG. Hopefully this was just a one-time incident. Gregg and I already knew how much we loved our Ola, but going through this horribly frightening time, not knowing if something was seriously wrong with her, made it even more clear to us how very much we love OUR baby girl. There is absolutely no doubt about her being ours! There is no difference in the love we feel for Ola just because she's adopted. The fact that she began and grew in my heart rather than in my body makes no difference in the way we feel about her.

Gregg and I are amazed with how far Ola has come. She is rarely afraid of anyone now. As a matter of fact she has turned into a bit of a "ham" She has a funny little personality! She is a happy, smiley, and very loving child. Her vocabulary is very good for her age and she talks a lot. We do not always understand what she is saying, but she talks a lot. Watching this active, confident, vivacious child emerge from the scared, leery, suspicious, withdrawn and angry baby that we first met has been so rewarding.

We cannot believe how much she has grown physically and socially. "Oh, what a little love can do?" My sister Missy say's "Ola can suck people in like no one she's ever seen." I think she is right. She has this "coy, flirtatious manner" that does seem "to reel her victim's right in." Not only does she love my sisters, but she has her uncles wrapped around her finger also. We are lucky to have a loving group of close friends that have also embraced her completely!

So far we do not seem to have any "bonding or adapting" problems going on. I worry a little about the way our family caters to her every whim and jumps to her every command. I tell my sisters, that we do need to discipline her at times, when needed, but they want nothing to do with that. Luckily, she doesn't need discipline much; she really is so sweet.

Ola today, much happier and more trusting!

"Neenee" holding Ola, playing with friends!

My father, the one I hardly remember being around when I was small, the one lacking so in patience, now melts into my daughter's hands. He swings her for hours without complaining. Holds her, rocks her, and reads to her for hours. I watch this completely puzzled, and it warms my heart. He tells anyone who will listen, in great lengths, all about her. This is amazing to me, being able to see my father in a very different light. Seeing my father as a "gentle, loving, and deeply caring" grandpa is a wonderful gift.

When we first met Ola, along with her "unhappy demeanor" she was also not very healthy looking. She was pale, had no hair, and was thin. She now has shiny blonde hair, rosy red cheeks, bright blue eyes, and a gorgeous "olive" complexion. She entertains us for hours and brings us so much joy. She is very playful and laughs easily. "Oh we have our moments", like every normal mother and her two-year old. We DO butt heads! I do not believe it is much different than it was with the boys when they were that age. Ola is stubborn and strong willed. Gregg and I tease about "how far we went outside the gene pool, hoping to weed out any bad traits like, stubbornness, tempers, overly strong wills, etc. It did not work; she still seems to have inherited some of those "not so great" traits anyway. However, for the most part, we could not feel more blessed.

Sometimes I am taken back when I look at her. I cannot believe how much she is my daughter. The love I feel for her, the pride, how much I hurt when she hurts, and the way she makes her "Ola" faces. The way she loves to dress up in pretty clothes, hats, and accessories and then runs out of her room to us, arms flung high in the air. "Tah dah", she squeals proudly. She is my girl!

As Ola became more and more secure with us I let myself feel less and less guilty about leaving her and started pursuing a few of my interests. I am able to pick back up some of the things I had put aside while we were searching for our daughter. Now that she is found and we have her home and settled we can all start to move forward with our lives.

Anyone who has children, whether by adopting or otherwise, knows what I am talking about. As new mothers, we all have to "acclimate" back into our lives. We slowly begin attempting to get back into balance, meeting our children's needs along with our own. It is not easy and continues on a daily basis as you raise them.

As I said before, I have never been very good at staying at home. I love people and like to be involved and busy with many diverse activities. I started working again at our local medical clinic as a "fill in" medical assistant. I recently signed up for a jewelry and metal smith class at a college. As I walked into my first class, I realized "I finally made it" to my Arts School! Although these classes may not lead me to the "glamorous" career I dreamed of 30 years ago, I am enjoying it immensely. I've embraced the fact that I'm happiest when I'm learning and experiencing new things. Before I started I struggled with all the reasons it would be "silly" to take this class, such as "it is too far to drive", "it's too expensive" and what if I suck at it"? Again, I stop to realize how easily guilt, self doubt and concern over what others might think; can have such "paralyzing" effects on a person. It can keep us "frozen" and unable to move forward. I think sometimes the decisions you make might not "make sense in your head", but make "perfect sense in your heart". Sometimes you just have to "go for it". It took so long for me to start really living my life my way, being a real "participant" instead of just "going along" trying to please everyone else. I like this new "unapologetic" way of living and hope my children learn this earlier in life than I did.

Before, we left for the Ukraine, I was also in the process of starting my own business, I did some research on becoming an "Officiant" or "Celebrant", something I had had an interest in for a long while. My love for writing and for sharing life led me to think I might really enjoy this, and hopefully be good at it. There also seemed to be a need for it in my area. I now write and perform wedding ceremonies, christening and commemorations.

I have really enjoyed this new opportunity. I devote a great deal of time to each ceremony. I write each ceremony individually so that it reflects the people whom I am writing it for. My ceremonies are "non denominational", which allows me the freedom to write the ceremonies to mirror individual beliefs. I tell my children that the foundation for my religious beliefs is simple, "just try your best to be a good person." I tell them that God gave us all good hearts and that if we stop and listen to them, "we will always know the right thing to do". Before each ceremony I say a prayer and I always feel God with me and feel calmer.

When you work in the medical field, it can be very draining. You care for the sick, injured, and sometimes the dying everyday. This of course can be difficult and depressing. I have enjoyed working as an office nurse for all these years so much, and probably will continue to work in the field in some way or another. However, I do have to admit it has been fun to share some of the more "joyful" times in people's lives for a change. Sometimes I help with selecting the music, decorating and catering. It really is fun watching it all come together and being able to be a part of these memorable times.

I do feel fortunate and blessed in every aspect of my life. We struggle to find our place in this world. I feel a little like I have come full circle, back to where I started, but with a different perspective. I hope that I appreciate everything more now. I look out my window at a grain bin that I remember my cousins and I putting together with my grandfather. What a tedious, boring, and hard job that was. But when the grain bin was all done we were all so proud of it! It is still there now and we still store our wheat in it. I look at it often and remember my grandpa and my childhood. When the boys were babies, and I'd been home a "few days in a row too many", more than once I met Gregg at the door and he would know by looking at me, I needed a break. I would zip out the door and drive to the top of the hill and park by grandpa's grain bin. It has the most beautiful view up there and is a "calming', relaxing place to me. Sometimes we would get a babysitter, drive up there together, and have a picnic! It's still my favorite "escape place" when I need one. I have asked to have my ashes scattered there when I die, because of the strong connection I feel there to the past, present, and future.

I am definitely not claiming my life is perfect now. It is not always easy living in such an isolated, rural area. Taking care of three kids, our home, and then trying to find time to do other things I enjoy, is a constant challenge. I am sure this is a very common problem shared by most women (and men too, I suppose).

My greatest loves are; theater, concerts, book stores, and going out to nice restaurants. I love to "dress up" and "go out", like Ola, only I rarely do the "tah dah" thing. We are far away from any of these things and I complain about it often. I try to remember the important things that I do have though. I have a husband who loves me, three beautiful, healthy children, and a wonderful place to raise them. I try to keep myself busy enough with work, and creative, productive projects. I believe that being happy and finding joy in your life is an on going and constant process. It is not always easy and it is different for each of us.

I have wonderful friends and family to lean on. I accept my strengths and my weaknesses. I accept that I am an "overly emotional" person and I have to work at processing "stress" in a positive manner. I have learned a lot about love, life, forgiveness, and understanding. I try to cut the people in my life "lots of slack" because we are all only human, each of us "doing the best we can". I try not to be a "perfectionist" because I believe most the time it is motivated by all the wrong things. I am learning not to worry about my house being spotless or perfect and to focus instead on my kids or doing things I enjoy. I try to surround myself with positive people, because this can affect your view on life more than anything can.

I can look at my mother and father and know now, that they did the best they could. I am sure they would change a few things if they could, as I know I would. Now that I am a parent, I do understand what a tough job it is. I am friends with my ex-husband and see how he has paid for his mistakes and hopefully learned and grown from them as I have. We are on good terms and I even write songs for his band! I try to remember the best of my childhood and chalk the rest of it up to "experience".

I appreciate now the incredible gift of "family". Although the "inner emotional conflicts" can be "oh so challenging" it is worth working through them. My sisters and I realize that although we sometimes hurt each other, when "push comes to shove" we are always there for one another. Now my Ola has that too. We help each other try to find the way. We are all very different, yet very much the same, whether we like to admit it or not. I am so grateful for each of them. Family is something we all take for granted at times, until we need each other. How sad it is when families hold grudges and stay angry at each other until it is too late.

When I visited the orphanage, I was so saddened to look at those beautiful and precious orphans and think that they had "no one". How could a child have no one? No one in the whole world to love them? How can that be? My daughter and my sons are the best thing that has ever happened to me. What miraculous, amazing blessings they are. When I look in my daughter's eyes now, I reflect on how far she has come. I reflect on how far I have come, and most of all, I reflect on how far we can go now, together.

Our family, complete now!

Epilogue

It was one year after we came home with Ola and my father was about to turn seventy. He kept talking about a family reunion in Ireland that he wanted to go to on his birthday. My mother hates to travel and did not want to go. At one point, I told him that if he wanted to "pay my way" I would go with him. I was sure he would never go for that. Much to my surprise, he said OK! I could not believe I was willing to travel again, let alone leave my kids for two whole weeks, and travel with my Dad! I decided that this would be a much different trip than our trip to the Ukraine and hopefully not nearly as stressful or emotional. I was very excited about going to Ireland, but a "small part of me" was worried about how Dad and I would get along. I think everybody was a little worried about it. I knew we had both grown up a lot and believed firmly we would be just fine. My father's mother's family had all come from Northern Ireland, and we still had many relatives there. Some of our family still lived on the original family homestead. This would be a wonderful time to reconnect with our family from there and also with each other.

Once again, Niki, along with my family and friends stepped in to help and I knew my kids would be well taken care of. Gregg encouraged me to go, so Dad and I decided to "go for it"! Therefore, off we went on our trip! We stopped first in Paris. We were amazed by the beautiful architecture, paintings, the Eiffel Tower, Notre Dame, the Louver and more. We took in a show at Moulin Rouge, which I adored. I thought of Natasha and our plan to meet here in one year. Coincidently, I'm actually in Paris almost exactly a year later! I emailed Natasha before we left to see if there was anyway she could meet us. Sadly, for financial and political reasons, it was impossible for her. We suspected that would be the case. "Someday", we will find away, we promise each other again.

Dad and I "jetted over" to London now! We enjoyed taking in sites like the Windsor Castle, and the Parliament. The first night we landed just in time to take in the "historical" Live 8 concert (July, 2, 2005). "Make history, wipe out poverty" signs were everywhere as it was the theme for this concert. All profits were going toward helping wipe out poverty and hunger in Africa. We were staying right by Hyde Park where the concert took place and although we could not see the stage, we could hear it very well in the outdoor "pub' next to our hotel.

It was exciting to hear that the likes of Madonna, Paul McCartney, Elton John, and others who were coming together for such a good cause. No matter what your political beliefs are, who could begrudge efforts to wipe out hunger? Again, as when we traveled to the Ukraine I was struck by how much we are all connected in the world. I admired these musicians, and everyone else involved in this project who feel obligated to help these poor starving children. It is good and right to care about the suffering, especially when they're children. Each and every one of us, in our own small way, CAN make a difference.

We went from feeling like we were a part of something very positive, however, to getting way too close to being victims of the very negative. We went from watching people motivated by love to watching people motivated by hate! We got out of London just hours before terrorists bombed buses there. When I first caught the news on TV in Ireland, it really shook me up. Dad and I could have easily been there. We had just been on some of those same buses, in the "tube" and underground of London just hours before the bombings.

It was awful, knowing it could have been us. Immediately I thought about my kids and how "unimaginable" it would be to never see them again. I felt guilty about being away from them and for a while, thought I should catch the next flight home. We watched with the rest of the world in horror as London tried to help the injured. I felt so bad for the families as they anguished not knowing where their loved ones were. I didn't realize my own family was doing the same thing. I desperately wanted to call home at this point, but was not anywhere that I could use a phone.

Gregg was not sure where we were. He thought we were in Ireland, but looking at our itinerary he could not be positive we had made it out of London. Gregg checked with the hotel where we were going to be staying in Ireland, but we had not checked in yet. Through a series of "hits and misses" it took hours for us finally to connect. Gregg had really started to panic. When I heard his voice on the phone, it was really shaky. We had a very emotional, loving conversation, and it was hard for me to not catch the next plane home.

Driving from Dublin to Northern Ireland proved to be the most difficult time for Dad and me. Driving on the very narrow roads, not to mention it was the "wrong side of the road" for me, and the fact that everyone in Ireland drives VERY fast, made for stressful driving conditions. We learned later that there are more people killed on the road from Derry to Carndonaugh than anywhere else in the world. I have no problem believing this. We also witnessed the tension between the IRA and the British loyalists first hand when we went through Derry. There were army tanks and soldiers in full gear everywhere, apparently in case the protests that happened this time of year got out of hand. This only added to my apprehension. I was reminded that, unfortunately, there seems to be no place in the world that is not affected in some way by hatred and violence.

There were a few "close calls" driving, a couple of detours, and a few wrong turns, which put my short-fused father over the edge. Unfortunately, my dad does not realize that screaming and cursing does not help the driver navigate whatsoever. By the time we reached our destination, of Carndonaugh, I was in tears. Dad had no idea how much his yelling had upset me. I began to remember why I had left home at 16. I was grateful to "dump" my dad off with our Irish cousins at the local pub and go back to our hotel to "regroup"! Combining the rough drive my Dad and I had had along with my homesickness for Gregg and the kids I was having a hard time and really wanted to just go home. This is when it all came back to me. I had to remember how I need to separate the father that I love from the ugly temper that I hate again. I had to remember that If I can do that, we will be OK. I had to remember how he is with my Ola and the boys. I had to remember all the things I love about him and get past that temper that I hate and that hurts the ones he loves so much! Dad came in later that night and had had a great time with our Irish cousins. He had "no clue" of the "emotional struggle" I had gone through that night. Some things never change....or had they? I had some how, some where, learned to cope better, with my Dad....with life! Luckily by the next day, I had managed to recover and decided to enjoy the rest of our vacation.

Ireland was so beautiful. Our family that lives there, along with all the cousins who had traveled there for the reunion, were amazing people. They were so open and friendly and showed us such a good time in Ireland. It was a very sentimental time as we saw the original family homestead and heard wonderful stories about our ancestors.

My favorite story was the trunk story. Apparently my great grandfather was reluctant to propose to my great grandmother so she had given up and decided to pack up all of her belongings and head to America, where she would be able to get a teaching job. There were very few opportunities for women in Ireland at the time. With her trunk already loaded onto the ship and she herself just about to get on board, my great grandfather showed up just in time to finally propose to her. She stayed and married him, but her trunk full of all her belongings went onto America without her. It took her over a year to finally get her trunk of precious mementos back. Our family in Ireland still has possession of the trunk. I took a picture of Dad kneeling beside it on the old family farm in Carndonaugh.

We got goose bumps many time as we "went back in time" and reflected on our family history. The story of the "reluctant proposal" tickled me and reminded me of my own husband's reluctance to marry. Gregg had no problem proposing, but thought a five-year engagement was a good idea! I, of course, had a problem with this! He did finally manage to "set a date" and by the time we made it to our wedding day, we both happily and easily made our commitment to each other. Hearing all the stories and seeing the places where they occurred made our trip there wonderful. Dad preferred to do more of the organized sightseeing and not miss any of the parties. I preferred adventuring out on my own, with my map in hand and NO cursing copilot! I meandered through all the coastal villages and saw the most beautiful countryside I'd ever seen in my life. Ireland is just like the postcards. It is so very green and the people are jovial and fun. It was a very reflective, thought-provoking, and soul-searching time for me. Dad and I shared many special moments together, and I am eternally grateful for them.

Dad and the infamous trunk in Ireland

Dad and I both had a wonderful, memorable time. We managed to make it home safely and still friends. I know we are closer because of the experience. None of us are perfect, and getting along is not always easy. My dad is the funniest, most energetic, and passionate person I know. I am grateful for the wonderful time we spent together and proud of the fact we have managed to form the relationship we have now.

With time flying by so quickly, and each generation replacing the other, I believe we all need to realize, that love is the only thing that goes on forever. After witnessing first-hand just some of the conflict around the world, I still believe the kind and generous people far outnumber the mean and cruel. I do think that with a little more love we can stomp out hatred and violence. We need to start first as individuals and then form a united front all across the world. In my journeys I have learned how important it is to not judge so much and to reach out more. If we can try just a little harder to help each other along the way, pick each other up when we fall, (and we ALL do fall sometimes), the world would be a better place. Our lives are all intertwined, whether we are connected by heritage or in our hearts.

Personally, my search to find myself is ongoing and I think it always will be. I'm grateful to have a husband who gives me a lot of space and freedom to constantly explore the world and myself. I have a strong need to continue to grow, learn, and do new things. He reminds me all the time that we do not need anyone's permission or blessing to live our lives our own way.

The most important thing to both my husband and me is our children. Hopefully, as they watch their mother constantly out there searching, they will see and learn that there is a great big beautiful world out there and it is OK to get out there and explore it! I hope we can show them how to kick down the walls and be comfortable going outside the "boundaries" people will try to lay out for you.

Let there be no limits to what they can achieve as they begin their search to find themselves. For even if we can't be physically beside them, every single step of the way, we are always behind them, and with them in spirit. In finding myself and in finding my daughter, I have learned that family holds a place in our hearts that stays with us always and forever. May all of our children gain great strength from this.

About the Author

Cheryle Rietmann (known as Shelly to family and friends) lives in rural eastern Oregon on a wheat ranch with her husband Gregg, their two sons, Tanner and Evan and their daughter Ola. Shelly works part time as a Medical Assistant at a local clinic and manages her own business as a" Ceremony Officiant. Shelly enjoys writing in many forms, including song lyrics, weddings, christenings and also plays, along with directing. Shelly and her husband host an annual Blues Festival at an outdoor Amphitheater they built with their small community. A self proclaimed "artist wanna be", Shelly actively pursues those interests. Her and her husband are very involved with their children's school and sports activities. There family enjoys many outdoor recreational activities together. Shelly loves to entertain which usually means cooking for a large group of family and friends! Shelly and Gregg are huge adoption advocates!

978-0-595-36949-2
0-595-36949-9

Printed in the United States
57713LVS00002B/4-9